DE PROPRIETATIBUS LITTERARUM

edenda curat

C. H. VAN SCHOONEVELD

Indiana University

Series Maior, 11

THE NET
OF HEPHAESTUS

*A Study of Modern Criticism
and Metaphysical Metaphor*

by

DAVID M. MILLER

1971

MOUTON

THE HAGUE · PARIS

LIBRARY OF CONGRESS CATALOG CARD NUMBER: 70-154528

Printed in The Netherlands by Mouton & Co., Printers, The Hague.

ACKNOWLEDGMENTS

My thanks are due the following publishers for their generous permission to quote from works for which they hold copyrights.

Basil Blackwell, W. B. Stanford, *Greek Metaphor*.

Doubleday & Co., H. G. Henderson, *An Introduction to Haiku*.

Harcourt, Brace Jovanovich Inc., I. A. Richards, *Principles of Literary Criticism* and *The Meaning of Meaning*; T. E. Hulme, *Speculations*; Cleanth Brooks, *The Well Wrought Urn*.

Indiana University Press, Philip Wheelwright, *Metaphor and Reality*.

Alfred A. Knopf, Inc., Wallace Stevens, "Someone Puts a Pineapple Together".

Lear Publishers, Inc., I. A. Richards, *The Foundations of Aesthetics*.

New Directions Press, William Empson, *Seven Types of Ambiguity*; John Crowe Ransom, *The New Criticism*.

Oxford University Press, I. A. Richards, *The Philosophy of Rhetoric*; H. J. C. Grierson's edition of the poetry of John Donne.

Scribner & Sons, Susanne K. Langer, *Feeling and Form*.

Peter Smith Ltd., Allen Tate, *The Man of Letters in the Modern World*.

University of Kentucky Press, W. K. Wimsatt, *The Verbal Icon*.

University of Minnesota Press, Murray Krieger, *The New Apologists for Poetry*.

University of North Carolina Press, Cleanth Brooks, *Modern Poetry and the Tradition*.

And to the editors of *Language and Style* special thanks for permission to reprint "The Location of Verbal Art" which appeared in their journal in a somewhat different form.

PREFACE

In the eighth book of *The Odyssey,* Demódokos tells the story of the cuckolding and revenge of Hephaestus. Finding the sooty hands, lame foot, and ugly visage of her husband not to her taste, Aphrodite formed a liaison with the handsome Ares. The shameless pair met in Hephaestus' own bed, and the adultery was reported to the husband by Helios, god of the sun. On his anvil, Hephaestus formed a wonderful net, absolutely unbreakable and as light as cobweb. This net he placed above the bed and pretended a journey to Lemnos. When the lovers took advantage of his absence, they were imprisoned in the net, and the returned Hephaestus called all the gods to view their shame. There was laughter in Olympus at the discomfiture of Ares and Aphrodite, but Apollo and Hermes agreed that chains three times as heavy would not be too great a price to pay for lying 'beside the pale-golden one'. Reparations were guaranteed by Poseidon, and the lovers were released.

Although Homer does not say so, it is Hephaestus who is shamed. His marvelous net arrested for a moment the coupling of love and war, but the passion, attraction, and beauty escaped, and Hephaestus was none the less crippled or sooty. Such, it seems to me, is the plight of the critic. Whatever the virtues of the net he spreads to catch a poem, the essence escapes, and he is left in wonder at the inviolability of art, to return eternally to the forge of his systems to catch with reason the arational.

My purpose in mending a set of nets forged by our age of criticism is not to enable them, at last, to catch the essence, but in the hope that, like Hephaestus's net, they may expose to view the glorious couplings which only the poet can manage. The critics and works which I have selected for discussion form what seems to me to be the center of critical effort in the first half of the twentieth century. 'The New Criticism', as Ransom named it, has many virtues. Without lapsing into an academic game of explication, the New Critics were able to examine in

great detail the stimuli which the poet organizes. And their learning and
sensibility have changed for our time the WAY a poem means as well as
WHAT it means. Although new nets are now needed, the old ones have
taught us a great deal. My effort is to systematize what they have accomplished in order that we may profit from both their virtues and
defects.

Inevitably someone else would have made a different selection. New
Criticism without T. S. Eliot may seem at first to be incomplete. But
the syncretic nature of the New Critical effort and its resistance to
dogma makes any selection both arbitrary, and, in a sense, complete.
If a master smith must be named, I. A. Richards gets first call, both
because of the volume and quality of his writings and because even
later critics who disagree with him feel obliged to use his work as an
anvil. The skein I follow is the age-old problem of the split between
objective and subjective: art as a world of its own versus art as the
creation of the perceiver. It is the central theoretical problem which
bothers each of the New Critics, even underlying their troubles in
purely 'practical' criticism.

The particular item I focus on is metaphor, in theory and explication.
And the metaphysical poetry of the seventeenth century provides most
of the test cases for metaphoric theory. It is the poetry which the New
Critics saw as the highest reach of art. The choice is, I think, logical –
not only because the New Critics so often explicated the poems of
Donne, but also because in metaphysical poetry, metaphorical action is
so frequently responsible for the movement of the poem. It is at once
both subtle and obvious: subtle in its manifold interactions of tenor
and vehicle, and obvious because without a fairly sophisticated awareness of the ways of metaphor, the great poems of Donne and Marvell
are either meaningless or trivial.

The problem of objective and subjective eventually boils down to
one very difficult question: 'What is a poem?' Where does it exist and
how does it have being? As we shall see, the rejection of poetry as
purely objective, or purely subjective, or purely intentional insists that
the poem 'happens' in the mind of the perceiver. But the affectivism
which such an assertion implies need not be wholly impressionistic and
idiosyncratic. For there are, obviously, more or less successful 'objective correlatives'. It is to the nature of the objective signals which
provide the occasions for subjective correlation that the New Critics
(and the following chapters) address themselves.

As a kind of carrot, I hold out the definition of verbal art set forth by René Wellek in *Theory of Literature*:

The work of art, then, appears as an object of knowledge *sui generis* which has a special ontological status. It is neither real (like a statue) nor mental (like the experience of light or pain) nor ideal (like a triangle). It is a system of norms of ideal concepts which exist in collective ideology, changing with it, accessible only through individual mental experience based on the sound-structure of its sentences. (page 144)

We shall return to this 'definition' in Chapter Five. It seemed necessary to coin or redefine a number of terms, I appologize in advance for the barbarisms. Each term is carefully defined as it first occurs in the following pages.

I wish to express appreciation for the encouragement and guidance given me by the late William Van O'Connor, to Professor Jay Halio for many suggestions, and to Professor C. E. Nelson for many hours of fruitful argument. A Purdue Research Foundation grant in the summer of 1967 allowed me to devote time and effort to putting this study in its present form. As always, my wife, Nancy, provided ideas, indispensable patience and proofreading.

CONTENTS

CONTENTS

I

I. A. RICHARDS AND T. E. HULME:
THE RHETORIC OF METAPHOR

> Our skill with metaphor, with thought is one thing –
> prodigious and inexplicable; our reflective awareness of
> that skill is quite another thing – very incomplete,
> distorted, fallacious, over-simplifying. Its business is
> not to replace practice, or to tell us how to do what
> we cannot do already; but to protect our natural skill
> from the interferences of unnecessarily crude views
> about it; and, above all, to assist the imparting of that
> skill – that command of metaphor – from mind to
> mind. And progress here, in translating our skill into
> observation and theory, comes chiefly from profiting
> by our mistakes.
>
> *The Philosophy of Rhetoric*

The systems of I. A. Richards are a bewildering maze of categories, divisions, subdivisions, and sub-subdivisions; yet, it is Richards who provides the basis for a view of metaphor which is particularly suitable for an age of philosophical doubt and perceptive relativity. Richards focuses attention upon the reader, rather than upon either the poet or the artifact, and it is with the meaning of a poem to the individual that our critics have addressed themselves. Perhaps a convenient entry to Richards' systems may be found in the fragmented thought of T. E. Hulme, for his insights are much more attractive than the massive systems of Richards, though it is to Richards' imposition of order that we must soon return. By interest a philosopher and by nature a poet, Hulme's two great friends seem to have been the artist Jacob Epstein and the philosopher Henri Bergson. It may be that Eliot's gnomic remark that only the poet can be the true critic is as true now as it was in Pope's day, but the early promise which Hulme gave of constructing valuable theory was ended by the chance of war in 1917, almost before he had begun. Bergson had predicted that Hulme would do something of importance in aesthetics, and despite the fragmentary nature of the work, he was not mistaken. It is possible to see in the siftings of

Hulme's manuscripts accomplished by Herbert Read and published as *Speculations*[1] a remarkable set of insights, undeveloped, which so recent a critic as Wimsatt[2] feels called upon to treat. Although Hulme's ideas contain a number of insurmountable contradictions, their value and attractiveness is clear.[3]

Hulme writes: "You could define art, then, as a passionate desire for accuracy, and the essentially aesthetic emotion as the excitement which is generated by direct communication."[4] Several ideas which are of importance not only for Richards, but for Empson, Tate, Brooks, and Ransom as well, are here implicit. Most important perhaps is the insistence upon accuracy as the aim of art, with a complementary denigration of scientific accuracy. Secondly, it is suggested that the aesthetic state is indeed 'phantom',[5] and that what is called aesthetic emotion differs not so much in kind as in quality from other emotional experiences. The passage assumes that art is communication, or at least that certain attempts at a particular kind of communication produce art. What, then, according to Hulme, is the nature of that communication:

Language has its own special nature, its own conventions and communal ideas. It is only by a concentrated effort of the mind that you can hold it fixed to your own purpose. I always think that the fundamental process at the back of all arts might be represented by the following metaphor. You know what I call architect's curves – flat pieces of wood with all different

---

[1] T. E. Hulme, *Speculations*, ed. Herbert Read (London, 1924). The effect of Hulme's personality and the varied receptions of his work is summarized in the introduction to *Further Speculations*, ed. Sam Hynes (Minneapolis, 1955). Attitudes toward Hulme ranged from adulation to scorn. A review of the biography by Michael Roberts (London, 1938) which H. A. Mason printed in *Scrutiny*, VII (1938), 215, suggests a composite view which is unfriendly but essentially accurate. "... Hulme was of importance almost exclusively as a stimulating influence, and was possibly more valuable in conversation than in his writings. Many of his dicta can be found in different settings in, for example, the work of T. S. Eliot. But these ideas are only valuable when worked out and properly defined. It is by the success of those who are known to have come under his influence that Hulme will be esteemed." Mason complains that Hulme "as a thinker ... was essentially an amateur".
[2] W. K. Wimsatt, Jr. and Monroe C. Beardsley, *The Verbal Icon: Studies in the Meaning of Poetry* (Lexington, Kentucky, 1954). William Elton, *A Glossary of the New Criticism* (Chicago, 1948), sees Hulme as a primary influence upon T. S. Eliot, but does not indicate his influence upon Richards.
[3] Hynes, *Further Speculations*, writes an introduction full of interesting gossip, but the works he collects add little concerning metaphor to those presented by Read. The chapter called "Literary Criticism" repeats many of the ideas which I have quoted from Read.
[4] *Speculations*, pp. 162-163. Future page references will be included in the text.
[5] I. A. Richards, *Principles of Literary Criticism* (New York, 1925), pp. 11 ff.

kinds of curvature. By a suitable selection from these you can draw approximately any curve you like. The artist I take to be the man who simply can't bear the idea of that 'approximately.' He will get the exact curve of what he sees whether it be an object or an idea of the mind. (page 132)

Here is the germ of Richards' division of language into the language of science and the language of poetry.[6] Hulme in an essay which Hynes has printed under the head "Notes on Language and Style" refers to 'the "counter" language of prose' and 'the "visual" language of poetry' (FS, pages 78-79), and creates a brilliant metaphor for the difficulty of accurate communications: "A word to me is a board with an image or statue on it. When I pass the word, all that goes is the board. The statue remains in my imagination" (page 82). Both metaphors suggest that language is an obstacle, not an aid, to artistic communication; it is something which must be grappled with and through the force of will subdued, bent, to a particular purpose. In the simplest terms, Hulme's artist finds the language general; he must make it specific.

The implication here is quite the opposite of what Ransom, for example, has taken the 'early' Richards to mean.[7] The language of science has exact definitions because its referents are not exact. The language of science deals with abstractions and artificially constructed norms. The language of poetry deals with Plato's world of imitations. Science may then have the rigidness of definition manifested in the Ptolemaic astronomy. It is not concerned with the uniqueness of each but with the rule for all. Poetry, however, since it deals with the baffling variety of the individual, must of necessity be inexact – though its inexactness is more exact than is the exactness of science. Since the language of science strives to eliminate the subjective – all that is most human – from a statement of the perceptive act, it is able to be inhumanly exact, but at the price of being humanly inexact.[8]

[6]   Kenyon Review, II (1940). Philip Wheelwright and Josephine Miles dislike Richards' division. Wheelwright insists that Richards is a villain for denigrating poetry as 'pseudo-statement'. More seriously, he denies that the business of criticism is with either the poet or the reader. It is, he says, with the poem. He then writes about (a) what the poem means to the author, and (b) what the poem means to a reader. Josephine Miles agrees with his attack on Richards, but the greatest part of her letter is an attack on Wheelwright.
[7]   John Crowe Ransom, The World's Body (New York, 1938), p. 155. As his later writings in The New Criticism (Norfolk, Connecticut, 1941) show, Ransom is in substantial agreement with Hulme and Richards on this point, but the term 'pseudo-statement' applied to poetry apparently blinded him to what Richards was saying. For his division of language see The New Criticism, pp. 43, 79, 93, and 293.
[8]   This idea has become almost the universal apology for poetry among the New Critics and their descendants. For statements of it see W. J. Ong, "The Meaning

Hulme thinks best in metaphors, and like Richards, the flaws in his thought are often the result of either the writer or the reader mistaking the metaphor for the actual: the symbol for the referent.[9] He presents the artistic process by means of this metaphor:

Suppose that instead of your curved pieces of wood you have a springy piece of steel of the same types of curvature as the wood. Now the state of tension or concentration of mind, if he is doing anything really good in this struggle against the ingrained habit of technique, may be represented by a man employing all his fingers to bend the steel out of its own curve and into the exact curve which you want. Something different to what it would assume naturally. (S, page 133)

But it is not his fingers which the artist uses to bend words from their flat meanings; it is other words. It is context which enables him to achieve the exact curve of meaning at which he aims. The importance of this distinction is that it makes words not only the recalcitrant material with which the artist struggles, but also the tool with which he accomplishes whatever bending is done.[10]

Secondly, Hulme's metaphor suggests that there exists prior to creation some aesthetic reality which the artist has but to copy. This second problem may be either the source or the result of the first. Hulme apparently feels the inadequacy of this attitude, for he shifts his metaphor. Now, rather than inanimate geometrical curves, words are thought of as subject to birth, decay, and death: "Every word in the language originates as a *live* metaphor, but gradually of course all visual meaning goes out of them and they become a kind of counters. Prose is in fact the museum where the dead metaphors of the poets are preserved" (S, 152).[11] Here again is a pre-Ricardian division of language, but there

---

of the 'New Criticism' ", *The Modern Schoolman*, XX (1943), 208, and Ransom, *The New Criticism*, p. 281. An interesting, more recent, statement is that of Philip Wheelwright, *Metaphor and Reality* (Bloomington, 1962), p. 128.

[9] W. J. Ong in "The Meaning of the 'New Criticism' " asserts that "the very connections of the strictest logical word are first, in some way or other, derived from material things and maintain always some commerce with the material ..." (p. 200). Ong at the same time sees Richardsmen as asserting against Cartesians the fundamentally metaphorical nature of all language.

[10] Hulme in *Further Speculations* seems to be approaching this idea, but he fails to state it clearly. Ransom's description of the functions of structure and texture (see Chapter Two, C, below) is perhaps the classical expression of this idea by the New Critics. Murray Krieger, *The New Apologists for Poetry* (Minneapolis, 1956), is in substantial agreement. For a discussion of Krieger see Chapter Three, C, below.

[11] Hulme, *Further Speculations*, more epigrammatically, says: "One might say that images are born in poetry. They are used in prose, and finally die a long,

is still a troublesome rolling together of things which might better be treated separately. The origin of words, the difference between prose and poetry, and the transmutation of one to the other is too much freight for the wheels. These three ideas, implicit in the passage from Hulme, must here be passed by in favor of a fourth implication: what is a 'live' metaphor? Hulme says that it is an image: "You get continuously from good imagery this conviction that the poet is constantly in presence of a vividly felt physical visual scene" (S, page 164). Again it might be objected that poetry for many people does not involve more than a very rudimentary visual image and that 'a vividly felt physical scene' is not only a mixing of metaphor, but also a generality so broad as to be of little use.[12] It may or may not be true, depending upon the definition of 'felt', 'visual', and 'scene'. It is interesting to watch Hulme apply pressure to the recalcitrant steel of words in an attempt to be explicit: "The thing that concerns me here is of course only the *feeling* which is conveyed over to you by the use of fresh metaphors. It is only where you get these fresh metaphors and epithets employed that you get this vivid conviction which constitutes the purely aesthetic emotion that can be got from imagery" (S, page 152). In this attempt to bend, two important insights emerge: the first is an implicit recognition that the nature of aesthetic communication is affective, 'the *feeling* which is conveyed over to you'; the second is the assertion that the central role in artistic communication is played by 'metaphors and epithets'. The first of these – the concern with the affective nature of artistic communication – is the central focus of Richard's work. *Princi-*

lingering death in journalists' English" (p. 75). Susanne Langer, *Philosophy in a New Key* (Cambridge, 1942), agrees, but sees the 'death' as useful, and, in many cases, desirable (p. 202).

[12] George Whalley, *Poetic Process* (London, 1953), presents an interesting distinction between idea and image: "In the sense I have been using the terms, an image is a perceptual entity which is most clearly to be understood in artistic activity; and an idea is a conceptual entity which is most clearly to be understood in analytical thinking. If an idea is introduced into poetic activity, it takes on something of the character of an image; and an image in technical activity will become an idea" (p. 136). Wheelwright, *Metaphor and Reality*, constructs a hierarchy: Image, Symbol, and Metaphor. Coleridge, *Biographia Literaria*, ed. J. Shawcross (London, 1907), suggests that image is the broadest of all terms. "It has been before observed that images, however beautiful, though faithfully copied from nature, and as accurately presented in words, do not of themselves characterize the poet. They become proofs of original genius only as far as they are modified by a predominant passion; or when they have the effect of reducing multitude to unity ... when a human and intellectual life is transferred to them from the poet's own spirit ..." (II, p. 16).

ples of Literary Criticism would, without affective aesthetics, fall in a heap. Even Richards' understanding of Coleridge is based upon affectivism. Some would say that the 'affective fallacy' is implicit in Richards' work from *The Foundations of Aesthetics* onward.

The second implicition, the realization that metaphor is the essence of artistic communication, is the core of Richards' most immediately useful work, *The Philosophy of Rhetoric*.[13] Although as the popularizer of affectivism Richards has had a profound effect upon the direction of modern criticism, it is his work on metaphor that is most widely useful to critics. Whatever their positions with respect to the objective-subjective conflict, the almost painfully obvious tools for metaphorical analysis which Richards gave to a series of convocations at Bryn Mawr are indispensable.[14]

Hulme was unable to work out a satisfactory way of talking about metaphors, but his perception of the atrophy of metaphorical qualities produced by continued familiarity is useful: "Metaphors soon run their course and die. But it is necessary to remember that when they were first used by the poets who created them they were used for the purpose of conveying over a vividly felt actual sensation" (*S*, page 151). This is certainly valid, but when he goes on to say, "You have continually to be searching out new metaphors of this kind because the visual effect of a metaphor so soon dies" (page 151), a problem arises. Metaphor is at least as non-visual as visual.[15] Here it may be hoped that Hulme was unconsciously using a metaphor – by visual effect he means vividness, whether that vividness be visual, tactile, auditory, or intellectual.[16] With this reservation, the statement carries us a good way toward a formularization of the purpose of poetry, according to Hulme:

[Poetry] always endeavours to arrest you, and to make you continuously see a physical thing, to prevent you from gliding through an abstract process. It

[13] I. A. Richards, *The Philosophy of Rhetoric* (Oxford, 1936).
[14] John Crowe Ransom, *The New Criticism*, adopts Richards' terms though he admits that he does not fully understand them (p. 67). Allen Tate as editor of *The Language of Poetry* (Princeton, 1942) acknowledges Richards as "the pioneer of our age in this field [semantics] of study" (p. viii). But he sees Richards' work as shifting from "psychology to philosophy". It would seem rather that Richards bases his philosophy on his psychology, and that he does not reject one in favor of the other.
[15] Whalley, *Poetic Process*, would agree: "The end of metaphor is not acute visual clarity, nor even is it intense sensory clarity; it is a process in which words and images are made incandescent and resonant" (p. 155). Whalley at times seems to go as far in favor of sound as Hulme does in favor of sight.
[16] Such does not seem to be the case, for Hynes quotes Hulme as saying, "by image I mean *Visual* image" (p. 79).

chooses fresh epithets and fresh metaphors, not so much because they are new, and we are tired of the old, but because the old cease to convey a physical thing and become abstract counters. ... Visual meanings can only be transferred by the new bow of metaphor; prose is an old pot that lets them out. Images in verse are not mere decoration, but the very essence of an intuitive language. Verse is a pedestrian taking you over the ground, prose – a train which delivers you at a destination. (pages 134-135)

Again, the reservation must be made. If Hulme means 'see', the theory will not hold; if, however, he is using a metaphor for vividness of affectiveness, then we may proceed. Two things require comment in this passage. The first is the nature of the imagery which is a 'bow', not a 'pot':

Fancy is not mere decoration added on to plain speech. Plain speech is essentially inaccurate. It is only by new metaphor, that is by fancy, that it can be made precise. (page 137)

By fancy, Hulme says he means an "analogy that has not enough connection with the thing described to be quite parallel with it ... it overlays the thing it describes and there is a certain excess ..." (page 138). The product of fancy, he suggests, is not quite a metaphor, for the unity which is achieved is not a result of the fusing heat of the imagination.[17] The second term which needs definition is 'intuition'. This apparently plays the same sort of role for the reader as the imagination does for the poet. To get at just what Hulme means by intuition, it is necessary to explore his interpretation of the Bergsonian intensive and extensive manifolds. Hulme constructs a theory of understanding, and, as usual, he does it with a metaphor ('plain speech is essentially inaccurate')[18]:

All sciences resolve the complex phenomena of nature into fixed separate elements changing only in position. They all adopt atomic theories, and the model of all the sciences is astronomy. In order to get a convenient nomenclature one calls all complex things which can be resolved into separate elements or atoms in this way "extensive manifolds." (pages 176-177)

The mind arrives at an understanding of extensive manifolds by divi-

---

[17] This is parallel to Ransom's idea of heterogeneity, *The New Criticism*, pp. 163 ff. See Chapter Two, C, below.

[18] Susanne K. Langer, *Philosophy in a New Key*, says that there is a kind of denotative language which is valuable. Language may become 'dead' through long and careless usage, but it may also be 'killed' for a special purpose: "Language, in its literal capacity, is a stiff and conventional medium, unadapted to the expression of genuinely new ideas, which usually have to break in upon the mind through some great and bewildering metaphor. But bare denotative language is a most excellent instrument of exact reason; it is, in fact, the only general precision instrument the human brain has ever evolved" (p. 201).

sion, by forcing relationships which do not exist, and by destroying the unity of the thing to be understood. "You have in your mind a model of what is clear and comprehensible, and the process of explanation consists in expressing all the phenomena of nature in terms of this model" (page 176). Today, it is brave if not wholly absurd to speak of 'all sciences'; the idea of the universe as being shaped like a tin can without dimensions or like an expanding inverted saddle can hardly be said to fit 'a model of what is clear and comprehensible'. But this is, for the purpose at hand, irrelevant. The idea of the 'extensive manifold' is a useful tool for examining literary criticism even though science may be neither so stupid nor so villainous as Hulme seems to suggest.

Opposed to this divisive process is another method of understanding. It is possible to view a whole *qua* whole, not simply as a temporary conjunction of parts:

One is to suppose rather an absolute interpenetration – a complex thing which yet cannot be said to have parts because the parts run into each other, forming a continuous whole, and whose parts cannot even be conceived as existing separately. It has differences, but these differences could not be numbered. It could not therefore be called a quantitative multiplicity, but a qualitative one. For the sake of convenience and the contrast with the other thing I prefer to call it an intensive manifold. (page 181)

Hulme describes the perception of an intensive manifold as being like the various pressures which a blind swimmer would feel if he were immersed in a swiftly moving, turbulent stream. The manifold is the sum of the sensations of pressure, indivisible into vectors. For the perceiver the intensive manifold results in an affective state, and the perception is gained not by analysis or ratiocination, but by intuition, which for Hulme is "the process of mind by which one obtains knowledge of an intensive manifold" (page 187).[19] This is, of course, circular. Intuition is what enables one to perceive an intensive manifold, and an intensive manifold is what one perceives by intuition. Yet it is possible to see the curve toward which Hulme is bending the steel. Intuition is a method of knowing, different from the analytical process involved in the perception of an extensive manifold, yet it is by no means mystical. It is a conscious, immediate perception of a complex unity as unity. Hulme here, as almost always, is too general to provide more than a provocative suggestion. He has divided the universe of perception into halves, but what of a poem? Richards develops these suggestions with

[19] Hulme thus anticipates Cleanth Brooks' condemnation of paraphrase. *The Well Wrought Urn* (New York, 1947), pp. 192 ff.

some degree of philosophical rigor and practical application. The 'Interinanimation' theory is the result.[20]

It is not difficult to see the connections between Hulme's division of perception and the functions which prose and poetry, in very general terms, play. Poetry attempts the intensive manifold, prose the extensive manifold. Richards follows this line of thought and classifies all language, with the exception of the jargon of science, as intensive manifold. Thus 'pseudo-statements' are the norm rather than the exception.[21]

And yet there is inherent in Hulme's usual diction the suggestion that both kinds of manifolds are external. The perceiving mind does not create. For Hulme the poet merely makes the spring of his words conform to a pre-existing reality, whether that reality be an emotion, an idea, or an image. The creative act is seen to take place prior to verbalization. It would seem necessary to make two important corrections before progress toward a grammar of metaphor can be accomplished. The first, which Hulme sometimes seems to grant, is that to a significant degree a section of the intensive manifold is within the mind of the being which perceives it ("the *feeling* which is conveyed over to you"). Such affectivism – as has been suggested – becomes the foundation of Richards' early work. A more systematic presentation would be hard to imagine. The second problem is one of which Hulme seems unaware: the degree to which words themselves participate in both poetic creation and perception – in the proddings which cause a single word to compound into a series of associations.[22] Although Richards notes this function, John Crowe Ransom in *The New Criticism* and Murray Krieger in *The New Apologists for Poetry* provide more lucid statements. The first problem may be discussed at once; it is the primary concern of the early Richards. The second problem must wait until Chapter Two.

In his first work I. A. Richards seems to take all knowledge as his province. Brief though it is, *The Foundations of Aesthetics*[23] lays the groundwork for far more than even so brilliant and prolific a mind as Richards' could be expected to accomplish in a lifetime. For the purpose at hand it is possible to pass over the seventeen kinds of THIS sub-

---

[20] *The Philosophy of Rhetoric*, pp. 47 ff.
[21] I. A. Richards, *Science and Poetry* (New York, 1926).
[22] Whalley, *Poetic Process*, condemns Hulme for thinking of metaphor as a descriptive tool. But, in context, it is possible to see that Hulme meant by 'descriptive' something like Whalley's 'embodying the feeling of reality' (p. 141).
[23] I. A. Richards with C. K. Ogden and James Wood, *The Foundations of Aesthetics* (New York, 1925).

divided each into the fifteen kinds of THAT; it is enough to note that a mind raging for order has set to work on the disorderly mass of aesthetic perception. The tone is confident, the manner arrogant. In 1922, Richards seems to have been firmly committed to a view of both external and psychic realities as 'extensive manifolds'. Still, it is easy to see some of Hulme's reverence for intuitive communication:

We normally react to our surroundings in ways which are labelled and classified in language, as stereotyped names. Thus grass is green or death is the end of life. In order, however, to react freely before a subject we must endeavour to be as little influenced by our habitual selections and attitudes as possible, – and this in the interest of representation itself . . . . What has been reproduced is what is affecting the artist and nothing else, nothing dragged from some other context or irrelevant experience ... but ... in every visual act we unavoidably bring to bear much of our experience. The artist selects in virtue of the impulses which his past life has developed in him. When we look at his work we shall in many cases miss much that is essential unless we are able to react with similar impulses. To do so is necessarily to involve our past life. (*FA*, pages 30-31)

The insistence at the beginning of the passage on a fresh perception might have been written by Hulme: there is the same concern for the numbing quality of the familiar, the same recognition of the inability of WORD to represent THING satisfactorily. There is even an insistence upon a specificity of experience which limits the poem – in composition. But before the passage ends, we are firmly within the Ricardian world. Once he begins to speak of the poet's impulses and the necessity and impossibility of the reader's duplication of those impulses, he is on the way to some system of objective correlative, though at greater length and with less piquancy than Eliot. There is here, too, something which Hulme did not perceive: each reading of a poem is unique, even if the readings are done successively by the same individual. "To react with similar impulses" is necessarily "to involve our past life", and a previous reading of the poem is of that past. The chimeras of external aesthetic qualities are dissolved, and the marish of impulse psychology lies ahead. From this passage grows the entire system of *Principles of Literary Criticism*.

Since it is through his organization of psychic impulses into synaesthesia that Richards arrives at his formulations concerning metaphor, it is necessary to follow the impulse theory, but an attempt has been made to stay near the shore and on the side of the interinanimations of *The Philosophy of Rhetoric*. "It is plain that a description of what happens when we feel aesthetic emotion (if ever we do) would fall into two halves. There would be a long psychological story about the organization of our impulses and instincts and of the special momentary setting of them due to our environment and our immediate past history on the one hand" (*FA*, page 63), and on the other hand, "a physico-physiological account of the work of art" which Richards does not develop and which need not be treated here. Generally he seems to include the physical condition of the perceiver as a part of the impulse and instinct organization which makes the perceiver more or less receptive to a poem. If one thinks ahead to the division of metaphor which Richards is to accomplish – the tenor and vehicle in conflict producing a third entity, an 'intensive manifold' – it is possible to see that he is here developing the same idea, but that his attention is focused, not only upon an external, perceivable verbal construct, but also upon the internal situation, the special momentary setting of tenor and vehicle in the mind of the perceiver.

To do this he uses the terms of speculative psychology. "There is good reason to deny that emotion is ever the result of the stimulation of merely one impulse. It seems to be due always to the interaction of the many" (*FA*, page 65). Here we have the germ of 'interinanimation' and 'plurisignification'; all that is required is for Richards to find a suitable external vehicle for statements which he realizes are concerned with psychic phenomena. As he is to discover in *The Philosophy of Rhetoric*, the nature of metaphor is such as to furnish that vehicle with maximum precision. He there holds out a partial understanding of the operation of metaphor in language as the first step toward an understanding of the processes of the human mind. Although he did not consciously think so at the time of writing, the comments on the activity of psychic impulses which fill *The Meaning of Meaning*[24] may be usefully taken as a metaphorical statement of the operations of metaphor, just as he later consciously takes the comments on metaphor as a metaphor for psychic phenomena.

The basic confusion which results when Richards' systems are applied practically arises from the impossibility of separating the external from the internal. A metaphor does not exist until it is perceived;[25] that perception Richards labels 'synaesthesis':

[24] I. A. Richards with C. K. Ogden, *The Meaning of Meaning* (London, 1923).
[25] Susanne K. Langer, *Feeling and Form* (New York, 1953), expresses the opposite view of the location of a poem. "The feeling expressed by this form [poem] is neither his [the poet's], nor his hero's, nor ours. It is the meaning of the symbol. It may take us some time to perceive it, but the symbol expresses it at all times, and in this sense the poem 'exists' objectively whenever it is presented to us, instead

As descriptive of an aesthetic state in which impulses are experienced together, the word, *Synaesthesis* . . . conveniently covers both equilibrium and harmony . . . . In equilibrium, there is no tendency to action, and any concert-goer must have realised the impropriety of the view that action is the proper outcome of aesthetic appreciation. (*FA*, page 75)

The first idea, here, is familiar. Hulme would have called it the "intuitive perception of an intensive manifold". But the passive nature of the aesthetic experience requires some further explanation. According to Richards, Man is constantly bombarded by impulses – many of them wholly contrary – the fulfilling of any of which necessarily frustates the accomplishing of many others. Since the usual way of fulfillment is by action and since the number of actions is temporally, spatially, and sociologically limited, Man must constantly be reduced from his potential – frustrated. Art provides an opportunity to experience a psychic fulfillment of impulses which if overtly expressed would be destructive. But such fulfillment is passive only insofar as the actions are not overt – not external. Psychic action is different from but no less intense than overt action. At the same time the peculiar timelessness of the aesthetic experience enables Man to experience conflicting impulses simultaneously without the social or physical short-circuit which would result if such experiences were overtly achieved. The account is not so fully developed as this in *The Foundations of Aesthetics*, yet even such a brief passage as the following quotation implies the entire system. The sequential development of Richards' ideas is perfectly logical:

In conclusion, the reason why equilibrium is a justification for the preference of one experience before another, is the fact that it brings into play all our faculties. In virtue of what we have called the synaesthetic character of the experience, we are enabled, as we have seen, to appreciate the relationships in a way which would not be possible under normal circumstances. Through no other experience can the full richness and complexity of our environment be realized. The ultimate value of equilibrium is that it is better to be fully than partially alive. (*FA*, page 91)

The messianic tone which offends many is very clear here, as is the sense of the necessity for arriving at a value judgment among examples of art. The implication is that the more complex the reaction to a work of art, the better. If the aesthetic quality resides in the mind of the

---

of coming into being when somebody makes 'certain integrated responses' to what a poet is saying . . . . For the poem is essentially something to be perceived, and perceptions are strong experiences that can normally cut across the 'momentary trembling order in our minds' resulting from assorted stimuli – whether comfort and sweet air, or cold and dreariness and cabbage" (p. 211).

perceiver (as Richards insists it does), and if the mind of the perceiver is more 'alive' with a complex equilibrium than with a more simple one, then it follows that the occasion for the equilibrium – the stimulus which becomes in the mind an aesthetic experience – must be capable of multiple interpretations. It must, in short, be ambiguous[26] if it is to provide the conflicting stimuli which are necessary for balance rather than decision. Strictly speaking, the stimuli neither agree nor conflict: the battles and their resolutions take place within the mind of the reader.

Before he was able to discuss so narrow a subject as metaphor – and broad as metaphor seems, it is but a single manifestation of the forces and qualities with which Richards is concerned in his early work – Richards felt the need to come to terms with the puzzles inherent in perceptive theory. To understand the value of his later, more practical contributions to a theory of metaphor it is necessary to trace in general terms his understanding of 'object', 'subject', and 'symbol'. The general problem he faces in *The Meaning of Meaning* may be illustrated prosaically: First, before perception is possible, there exists something to perceive – the physical object DOG. The first stage of perception requires that the dog be noted as different from the stimuli which surround him. The image of a particular dog is transmitted to the mind for interpretation; then, the general quality of 'dogness' suggested by the recurrence of similar sense perceptions is abstracted and stored in the memory. We now have a Referent and a Reference. Next, a symbol is constructed: visual and linguistic. There is the mimetic image of DOG which a photographer (and in more complex fashion, the visual artist) produces. And there is the linguistic symbol (for the most part inherited[27]), d-o-g, which must be considered as both an oral and a visual construct. We now have the three elements of perception: Referent, Reference, and Symbol. Further, it is necessary to consider the modifications of all three which occur when the initial contact is with the

---

[26] Wheelwright finds 'plurisignification' a more satisfactory term than 'ambiguity'. 'Ambiguity' means 'either-or', whereas plurisignification means 'both-and'. Ambiguity is looseness in literal language. Plurisignification is "a controlled variation and plurality of reference in language that deliberately transcends the literal". See *Kenyon Review*, II (1940), 266. Richards' 'poetry of inclusion', Brooks' 'irony and paradox', and Tate's 'tensive language 'are terms which point in the same direction.
[27] There is a basic fallacy in the method of critics who may be called semantic anthropologists. However sun GOT its name in the pre-dawn of history, the fact is that we learn its name by someone pointing and saying, "That's the sun". To know the 'history' of words is useful, to understand that they may well have personal associations is essential.

linguistic symbol rather than with the physical object: how, for example, does Cerberus differ from Spot who lives next door? And in addition, Richards insists that the initial process of perception is never from specific to general, but from general to specific. The mind may then produce a second generalization which requires three steps. The process goes from General, to Specific, to Abstract.[28] There is, of course, an interweaving of general-to-specific and the specific-to-abstract, just as there is instinctively a mixture of induction and deduction in thought.

The Meaning of Meaning contains a diagram which summarizes these perceptive relationships as Richards understood them in 1923.

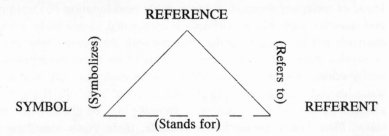

For the purpose at hand this diagram is useful chiefly to illustrate what the process of reading a metaphor is not.[29] Many of the relationships are at most only tangentially related to the specific problems of poetic analysis through an understanding of metaphor. For example, if we agree with Richards that poetry is designed to produce an attitude or state, rather than a belief or action, we may avoid the concern over the relationship between Symbol and Referent. It is very easy to become confused over the relationship between TRUTH and FACT. Once they enter the aesthetic realm, Cerberus and Spot may be treated as equally truthful, though not equally factual. The direct relationship between Symbol and Referent, which Richards admits does not exist and which is therefore putatively represented by a dotted line, need not be given even so ghostly a consideration. The right leg of the triangle may be thought of as indicative, in a very general way, of the process of poetic creation: the stimuli which cause the poet to produce an artifact. But since this study deals with the perception, rather than the creation, of metaphor, the right leg of the triangle is, in a sense, moved over to the left leg. Richards' basic triangle is thus reduced to a single line: that is,

---

[28]   W. J. Ong, "The Meaning of the 'New Criticism' ", spells this out in traditional terms. His example is the progressive elimination of possible meanings from the word 'man' if it is first encountered as a total abstraction.
[29]   I. A. Richards, *The Meaning of Meaning*, p. 11.

the perception of an artifact is really the perception of a symbol rather than a referent. There is still, however, a flow in both directions – from symbol to reference and from reference to symbol.

Yet rather than making the problem of understanding simpler, this collapsing actually produces further difficulties. Since on the literal level the aesthetic symbol (the metaphor) has become for the reader a referent, the metaphor must at the same time symbolize a thought and be that to which the reference (suggested by the symbol) refers. To complicate matters, the neat division between external and internal reference which accounts for personal idiosyncracies of perception has been very nearly collapsed. When a metaphor is read, all but the most literal elements of the referent – all but the marks of black on white – must be within the mind of the reader. Since the symbol, even in the relatively simple case of ordinary perception, has no direct relationship to the referent, the peculiar situation of poetry is that the very thing which initially seems to be the referent, the marks on the page, turns out to have no real connection with the actual reference. Thus the real stimuli of poetic perception are within the mind of the reader prior to his reading the metaphor. The marks on the page can only suggest a new combination of references. Therefore, the actual referent is of the same nature as the reference which is constructed as a result of aesthetic perception. It differs from the reference produced as a result of the stimulation of the symbol only in that it has been stored from an earlier act of perception. This earlier stimulus may have been produced as a result of perception of literal, objective referents, but more often than not, the stored references which are available for recombination as the result of aesthetic (poetic) stimulation have themselves been produced by anterior aesthetic perception.

In the peculiar aesthetic situation of poetry, then, it is the function of the marks on the page to recall from memory previously recorded references. Or in more palatable form: to provide occasions which demand fresh combinations of the references which the mind has in some manner stored.[30] To read is "to involve our past life". Since each

30 Susanne K. Langer, *Feeling and Form*, suggests an alternative. "The Black Beast of which most aestheticians who hold a theory of art as expression stand in fear is the concept of the Art Symbol. The unavowed fact which haunts them is the fact that an expressive form is, after all, a symbolic form .... The first crucial problem that finds solution [once this fact is accepted] is, how a work of art may be at once a purely imaginative creation, intrinsically different from an artifact – not, indeed, properly a physical 'thing' – yet be not only 'real', but objective. The concept of the *created* thing as nonactual, i.e. illusory, but imaginatively and

new combination is at least vestigially available for all future readings, and since elements other than perception are granted influence, Richards' system is not just the mind as a vast computer, certainly not as an idiot with a photographic memory. But perhaps one important factor does not get enough attention in Richards' system; the mind is able to a certain degree to choose and suppress among possible results of any particular stimulus. The mind, though perhaps unable to create from nothing at all, is quite capable of inversion, distortion, and finally of refusing to think about the issue at all. Richards gives too little space to the Will.[31]

Before Richards' speculations on the perceptive act involved in reading could get far, he had to realize the limitations of his triangle. Since the symbol of (word on paper) does not occupy the mind of the reader, but his attention is instead focused on the REFERENCE TO (re-called idea), a very large part of the significant referent, as opposed to the literal referent, must be internal. The affective nature of poetic communication becomes clear. The effect of a poem must differ in important ways because a part of its symbol must necessarily differ for different readers. The Ricardian triangle does well enough for the analysis of extensive manifolds, but since its method is division, it must fail to account for the intensive manifolds – and metaphors are the equivalent of Hume's turbulent, unvectorable stream.

Much of Richards' early work is obscured by excessive jargon. This is particularly true of his thoughts about 'engrams' – the stored percep-tions which symbols may recall: "An engram is the residual trace of an adaptation made by the organism to a stimulus. The mental process due to the calling up of an engram is a similar adaptation: so far as it is cognitive, what is adapted to is its referent, and is what the sign which excites it stands for or signifies" (MM, page 53). As a summary this serves very well; as exposition, it is terribly thick. The function of poetry "is to create ever more complex, non-repeated engrams". Since engrams are in part made up of subjective elements, discourse which attempts objectivity must avoid them as nearly as possible. For Richards, the worlds of science and the worlds of art operate by dif-ferent rules; the virtues of artistic communication become the vices of

---

even sensuously present, functioning as a symbol but not as a physical datum, not only answers the immediate question, but answers it in a way which suggests the answer to its corollary, the problem of technique" (p. 386).

[31] Mrs. Langer characteristically gives too much emphasis to the will – or per-haps her will is much stronger than mine.

scientific discourse.[32] Northrop Frye provides a more recent statement of the same idea in the essay, "The Archetypes of Literature".[33]

In *The Meaning of Meaning*, Richards begins to back into a discussion of metaphor. The nature of metaphor, he says, makes it possible for him to use it as an illustration for the process of abstract speculation:

In fact the use of metaphor involves the same kind of contexts as abstract thought, the important point being that the members shall only possess the relevant feature in common, and that irrelevant or accidental features shall cancel one another. (*MM*, page 214)

This is, in fact, not true, or rather it does not go far enough. Had Richards examined metaphor more closely he would have noted (as he later did) that features which at first appear to be 'irrelevant or accidental' actually play an important role in the operation of most metaphors. In *The Meaning of Meaning*, Richards is struggling with metaphor in the abstract; his examples are few and simple. His clearest statement of the nature of metaphor in that book is still far removed from "My love is a red, red rose."

Metaphor, in the most general sense, is the use of one reference to a group of things between which a given relation holds, for the purpose of facilitating the discrimination of an analogous relation in another group. In the understanding of metaphorical language one reference borrows part of the context of another in an abstract form. (*MM*, page 213)

In a later edition,[34] Richards recognizes the obscurantist nature of this definition. He sends the reader to "Chapter XXXII" of *Principles of Literary Criticism*, and there he is able to speak with greater firmness about the motor of poetry, metaphor. Yet rather than setting forth clearly illustrated principles upon which other critics could build, "Chapter XXXII" becomes a quagmire of impulse psychology. Impulses certainly exist and are important, but they cannot be diagrammed, unless the diagrammer constantly remembers that his diagram is only an illustration. The mistaking of symbol for referent is one of the greatest dangers to literary theory; Richards sometimes forgets his own warning.

But let us look at "Chapter XXXII":

It should not be overlooked that metaphor and simile – the two may be con-

---

[32] Although this idea is in all Richards' early work, *Science and Poetry* gives the fullest statement.
[33] Northrop Frye, "The Archetypes of Literature", *Kenyon Review*, XIII (1951), reprinted in *Fables of Identity* (New York, 1963).
[34] *The Meaning of Meaning*, eighth edition, footnote to p. 213.

sidered together – have a great variety of functions in speech. A metaphor may be illustrative or diagrammatical, providing a concrete instance of a relation which would otherwise have to be stated in abstract terms. This is the most common scientific or prose use of metaphor. It is rare in emotive language and in poetry. (*PLC*, pages 239-240)

There are several objections to be lodged against this passage. The simplest is a matter of terminology. The sort of 'prose-metaphor' of which Richards speaks might better be called analogy. The distinction is made clear by Henry W. Wells: "An analogy between two ideas is an assumption of similarity expressible as a general law. . . ." Although Wells admits that "it is not always possible to distinguish between metaphor and analogy",[35] the distinction is a useful one. In general terms, the difference is a parallel to that between exposition and illustration.

But a much stronger objection must be made. Either Richards' diction is imprecise, or he is denying the distinction between metaphor and simile. Though they are perhaps more like each other than either of them is like a third sort of thing, they are still quite different. The traditionalists who labor over the distinction in grammatical terms are preserving an important discrimination. "Like/as" and "is", if read with the attention which critics today demand of less structural elements of speech, are radically different. The first places one object beside another, analytically noting similarities and differences; the second places one object upon another and fuses the two into a single entity. In Hulme's terms a simile is an 'extensive manifold'; a metaphor is an 'intensive manifold'. It is only upon the level of a limited kind of paraphrase that the two are alike. Certainly anyone who will visualize "My love is a red, red rose" – can SEE the differences between a simile and a metaphor.[36] Of course it is true that many, perhaps most, meta-

---

[35] Henry W. Wells, *Poetic Imagery* (New York, 1924), p. 4.

[36] Among the critics who see no distinction between metaphor and simile is Philip Wheelwright, *Metaphor and Reality*, who gives two versions of Burns' line: "O my love is like a red, red rose", and "Love is a red rose". He concludes that the simile has 'more tensive life, more metaphoric vitality' than the metaphor. He cheats. The form of his metaphor is barren. Secondly, he seems to assert a hierarchy of imagery, even as he says that there is no substantial difference. His proof, if valid, would disprove his thesis. Wells, *Poetic Imagery*, calls the 'red, red rose' an Exuberant metaphor, by which he means that "two powerfully imaginative terms influence one another strongly, while their relationship remains vague and indefinite" (pp. 50-51). The New Critics have been ingenious in making the relationship between tenor and vehicle more than 'vague and indefinite'. Empson's work might lead Wells to reclassify Burns' line as an "Expansive Metaphor . . . characterized by the unloosing of a wide range of suggestion and the strong and mutual modification of its parts" (p. 33).

phors are not meant to be visualized, especially the example just noted, but it is in visualization that the distinction is most apparent. It holds upon all levels of perception, except that of the abstracting intellect.

Almost all similes may be read as if they were metaphors, for lurking in the shadow of every simile is a metaphor. This may be particularly true for readers brought up on 'close reading' of the text. But what of the similes of Homer and Milton? It seems important to know whether Satan leaped into the Garden of Eden in the shape of a wolf or merely as a wolf would leap. Or whether Athena takes the form of Mentor, or if Mentor on occasion is merely as wise as Athena. Perhaps Richards is saying that a simile which is not meant to suggest a parallel metaphor is rarely intense enough to work in "emotive language and in poetry". Even this is doubtful; it would seem that a poet who consciously chooses to state a relationship as a simile is purposely excluding certain 'interinanimations' that a metaphor would have expressed. And it might be well for the reader to be aware of the intended limitations of the comparison.[37] It would seem that simile is somewhere between metaphor and analogy: a simile does not fuse its elements as does metaphor, but neither are its assumptions of similarity necessarily 'expressible as a general law'.

Richards' statements concerning the nature of metaphor in *Principles of Literary Criticism* are clearer and more useful than those in *The Meaning of Meaning*.

[Metaphor] is the supreme agent by which disparate and hitherto unconnected things are brought together in poetry for the sake of the effects upon attitude and impulse which spring from their collocation and from the combinations which the mind then establishes between them. (*PLC*, page 240)

---

[37] W. B. Stanford, *Greek Metaphor: Studies in Theory and Practice* (Oxford, 1936), quotes classical critics from Aristotle to Longinus who say that metaphor and simile are differing forms of the same thing. He disagrees: "No: the finest type of metaphor transcends the explicitness of paraphrase. There is some quality in the greatest metaphors which distinguishes them entirely from simile. The difference between the two is very like that between prose and poetry. Simile, like prose, is analytic, metaphor like poetry is synthetic; simile is extensive, metaphor intensive; simile is logical and judicious, metaphor illogical and dogmatic; simile reasons, metaphor apprehends by intuition .... Thus while the lower types of each can be almost indistinguishable from each other, the purest products are of entirely different natures. Simile aims at explicitness and definition .... Metaphor defies reason and yet prevails .... Like poet and scientist they eternally disagree about methods and eternally agree about ultimate realities" (pp. 28-29). "Thus simile differs from metaphor fundamentally. Superficially, they are not unlike; in logical terms the simile says 'A B under certain specified conditions'; metaphor says 'A B in a whole universe of discourse' " (p. 30).

Once again Richards affirms the central function of metaphor, and his definition is formulated in terms of impulse psychology, but otherwise it goes little further than *discordia concors* and 'heterogeneous ideas . . . yoked by violence together'. The primary addition to these traditional conceptions of metaphor which Richards here makes is the result of his affective theory. There are two stages: collocation and connection. The artifact provides the one; the reader provides the other. But Richards is not yet primarily interested in metaphor. Just as he had to puzzle out the relationships involved in perception before he could deal with specific lines of poetry, so too he must try to assess the nature and function of impulses before he can turn his attention to the practical matter of metaphor. Note the typical shift of focus from the nature of metaphor to the nature of the mind which occurs in the following passage. Here for once it would have been valuable for Richards to have forgotten that his discussion of metaphor is but a metaphor for the operation of the mind:

There are few metaphors whose effect, if carefully examined, can be traced to the logical relations involved. Metaphor is a semi-surreptitious method by which a greater variety of elements can be wrought into the fabric of experience . . . . But what is needed for the wholeness of an experience is not always present naturally, and metaphor supplies an excuse by which what is needed may be smuggled in. (*PLC*, page 240)

This would seem to be the kernel of John Crowe Ransom's discussion of 'irrelevant texture'. And the suggestions about metaphor are intriguing, but Richards is not interested in the 'excuse', but in what is 'smuggled in'. When he follows this passage with: "Impulses which commonly interfere with one another and are conflicting, independent and mutually distractive are able to combine into a stable poise" (page 243) – we are dealing in impulse psychology, not in an analysis of the operation of metaphor. In order to understand Richards' presentation, it is necessary to examine, further but briefly, what he means by impulses.

Impulses are the basis for all art: "it is in such resolution of a welter of disconnected impulses into a single ordered response that in all the arts imagination is most shown" (*PLC*, page 245). Richards' perceptive theory has discovered beauty to be in the mind of the beholder; he is now trying to face the impossible, but seemingly necessary, task of following beauty from the world of object to the world of impulse. The basic premise of impulse psychology we have met earlier, but the ideas from Richards' earlier works are here expanded and clarified: "This balanced poise, stable through its power of inclusion not through the force of its exclusions, is not peculiar to Tragedy. It is a general characteristic of all the most valuable experience of the arts", and "we must resist the temptation to analyze its cause into sets of opposed characters in the object. As a rule no such analysis can be made. The balance is not in the structure of the stimulating object, it is in the response. By remembering this we escape the danger of supposing that we have found a formula for Beauty" (*PLC*, page 248). The danger is real and must be avoided, but there is a another danger of which Richards seems unaware: if 'balance' is wholly the product of the mind, then there would be equal opportunity to achieve this balance regardless of the nature of the object which serves as stimulus. The 'artifact' disappears.

As is often the case with real or imagined problems in Richards' systems, the answer appears in a later work. In the chapter of *Coleridge on Imagination* titled "The Wind Harp", Richards finds four meanings of nature.[38] The first of these four, "The influences, of whatever kind, to which the mind is subject from whatever is without and independent of itself" (page 157), must include the artifact. The fact that a rug or a jar may be on some occasions as 'aesthetic' as a sonnet does not destroy their objectivity. Any object under certain conditions is capable of stimulating impulses which may be organized into an aesthetic perception. Certainly 'balance' is a response, not a stimulus, but like the sophomoric question of the tree falling without a hearer and so making no sound, the problem is an illusory one based upon semantic confusion. The realist affirms that sound equals vibration; the projectionist that sound is perception of vibration. The tree makes no sound, but without the tree, the hearer cannot project the reaction SOUND into the vibrations, and within the tree there is potential for falling and so causing VIBRATIONS which may be projected as SOUND by a presence. The basic situation of art is parallel; just as some objects do not have the potential of vibrations which can be perceived as sound, so too there is within the artifact a greater or lesser potential for providing the kind of stimuli which will cause the mind to call up engrams which may then be organized as balance and so produce the state of being which Richards calls 'aesthetic emotion'.

Richards' explanation of the human mind sorting, ordering, and rejecting impulses in order to arrive at a balance rises to its most confident in *Principles of Literary Criticism*. Note the limitations and

---

[38] I. A. Richards, *Coleridge on Imagination*, 3rd ed. (Bloomington, 1960), first published (New York, 1934), p. 141.

pretensions to accuracy in a passage which may well be the immediate source of the many varieties of 'tension' theory in the New Critics:

There are two ways in which impulses may be organised; by exclusion and by inclusion, by synthesis and by elimination. Although every coherent state of mind depends upon both, it is permissible to contrast experiences which win stability and order through a narrowing of the response with those which widen it. A very great deal of poetry and art is content with the full, ordered development of comparatively special and limited experiences, with definite emotion, for example, Sorrow, Joy, Pride, or a definite attitude, Love, Indignation, Admiration, Hope, or with a specific mood Melancholy, Optimism, or Longing. And such art has its own value and its place in human affairs . . . . But they are not the greatest kind of poetry. (*PLC*, pages 249-250)

Note first the distinction which is basically that made by Hulme: inclusive-exclusive, though Hulme's external world has been transferred to psychic ground. Next note the listings of subcategories which imply scientific method. And finally, note the assertion of levels of poetry with the 'tensive' poetry at the top. In the 'higher' kind of poetry Richards tells us that impulses "are more than heterogeneous; they are opposed". They are such that "in ordinary non-poetic, non-imaginative experience, one or the other set would be suppressed to give as it might appear freer development to the others" (*PLC*, page 249). This opposition of impulses which are yet organized will bear 'ironical contemplation'. "Irony in this sense consists in bringing in of the opposite, the complementary impulses . . . irony is . . . constantly a characteristic of poetry which is [of the highest order]" (*PLC*, page 250). This is familiar and yet difficult. If it is granted that talking of the attributes or relationships in an entity which cause it to be called beautiful is difficult, it is hardly obvious that transferring these qualities to a mental set which is available only by means of introspection will make the task easier. Such, at least, seems to be the basis of Ransom's objection.[39] In his later work Richards resorts to the external world for analogies of the aesthetic experience, although he usually asserts that the experience is an internal phenomenon.

He is not, at the time of *Principles of Literary Criticism*, unaware of the difficulties inherent in an attempt to examine the aesthetic balance "Those opposed impulses from the resolution of which such experiences spring cannot usually be analysed . . . but sometimes . . . they can, and through this accident literary criticism is able to go a step further than the criticism of the other arts." But even when such is the case "we can

[39] Ransom, *The New Criticism*, p. 53.

only conjecture dimly what difference holds between a balance and re-conciliation of impulses and a mere rivalry or conflict. One difference is that a balance sustains one state of mind, but a conflict two alternat-ing states" (*PLC*, pages 250-251). It would appear that this adds little to what Coleridge says of metaphor. A good metaphor is one in which the two elements (with an almost unlimited number of characteristics on each side) fuse into a third.

Richards divides the contributors to the aesthetic state:

Among the causes of most mental events . . . two sets may be distinguished. On the one hand there are the present stimuli reaching the mind through the sensory nerves, and in co-operation with these, the effects of past stimuli associated with them. On the other hand is a set of quite different factors, the state of the organism, its needs, its readiness to respond to this or that kind of stimulus. The impulses which arise take their character from the interaction of these two sets. (*PLC*, page 262)

This sounds very mechanical; the mind has only to be the passive re-ceiver of signals from inside and outside the body and to recall from memory relevant data. But Richards is aware that the will itself has a good deal to do with the final perception of a work of art:

It is plain that the independent internal conditions of the organism usually intervene to distort reference in some degree. But very many of our needs can only be satisfied if the impulses are left undistorted. Bitter experience has taught us to leave some of them alone, to let them reflect or correspond with external states of affairs as much as they can, undisturbed as far as possible by internal states of affairs, our needs and desires. (*PLC*, page 263)

Here Richards refers only to the animal qualities of man which may interfere with the aesthetic operation, but it is possible to extend his warning to include irrelevant, contradictory, or unpleasant connotations of the artifact as well. Here Richards gives particularly good advice to the impressionistic reader, and such a passage might serve as a defense against those who accuse Richards of the 'affective fallacy'. If we extend 'internal condition of the organism' to include not only spots on the liver, but also the idiosyncratic associations which a stimulus calls forth in a particular reader, we have a restatement of the tradi-tional theory of decorum – with a difference. Usually we think of de-corum in reference to the creation of a poem; Richards is suggesting that the reader must be decorous in his creation of the poem.

Richards dismissed the question of 'truth' in the aesthetic experience as he speculated upon the triangle of perception in *The Meaning of Meaning*. In *Principles of Literary Criticism* he reaffirms that dismissal in terms which have, rightly, caused critics such as Tate and Ransom to rebel:

> It matters not at all in such cases whether the references are true or false. Their sole function is to bring about and support the attitudes which are the further response. The questioning, verificatory way of handling them is irrelevant, and in a competent reader it is not allowed to interfere. (*PLC*, page 268)

On the contrary, it matters a great deal whether poetry is true or false, and Richards knows it. What he means to say, it may be hoped, is that it matters not at all whether the elements of poetry are FACT or FICTION. And by 'true references' it seems clear that he means FACTS, not philosophic truths. Often, as here, the terms which Richards uses suggest that an experiment could test the reference, even though the passage literally says that such testing is irrelevant – in a scientific sense it is not only irrelevant, it is impossible.

The diagram on page 116 of *Principles of Literary Criticism*, though it is as curious as an antiquary's cabinet, indicates very well both the virtues and flaws of Richards' theory as it stood in 1925. Since the aid which Richards sought from practical psychology has not been forthcoming, the diagram has remained wholly imaginative. Such may or may not be the occurrences when we read "Arcadia, Night, a Cloud, Pan, and the Moon". As a recognition of the individuality of each reading of a poem, it is valuable. It serves as a corrective for those who try to isolate the whole of beauty in externals. And as a graphic indication of the probable complexity of the human mind engaged in art, it serves very well. But as 'fact' it is of no value. It may best be regarded as a graphic metaphor for Richards' abstract statements. In *The Philosophy of Rhetoric* Richards discovers a more successful metaphor to say much the same thing, and like all good metaphors, it takes on an independent existence until it is something far more than an illustration of affective-impulse-psychology. Richards, in handling the currents of mental electrical storms, produces a method of metaphorical analysis which has allowed modern critics to treat metaphysical poetry with understanding and some degree of precision.

The Philosophy of Rhetoric originated as a series of lectures delivered at Bryn Mawr College in 1936. Perhaps the requirements of oral presentation forced Richards to free his ideas from the turgid syntax and cryptic diction which vitiate his earlier work. Or perhaps the ten years which had passed since the conception of these ideas in *Foundations of Aesthetics* allowed him to revise and correct ideas which were imperfect in earlier statements. Whatever the reason, the summary and codification of Richards' method presented in the six lectures are his greatest achievement in criticism. Even though his remarks are not directed to literary critics, the basic statements of the nature of metaphor are so sane that no handbook of literary terms is complete without definitions of 'tenor' and 'vehicle'.

Richards begins the 'new' rhetoric with an examination of the initial act of perception. The agglomerative production of abstractions is not, he says, the first stage of perception. "A particular impression is already a product of concrescence. Behind, or in it, there has been a coming together of sortings" (*PR*, page 36). For example, when we note that a group of things are of the same genre, it is necessary that we have some method of perceiving their basic identities as separate units before we can note similarities which allow us to place them together. There are then, two kinds of abstractions. The first kind is non-ratiocinative, almost unconscious. The second is the kind we use in arriving at abstract categories. "Our risk is to confuse the abstractness we have thus arrived at intellectual with the primordial abstractness out of which these impressions have already grown – before ever any conscious explicit reflections took place" (*PR*, page 36). This is basically a restatement of the double process which Richards had noted in *The Meaning of Meaning*: first distinction, then abstraction.[40]

Richards, who earlier seemed to concentrate upon the internal segment of human perception, here makes a place for the stone which can be kicked. Rather than a reversal, however, it is a correction of emphasis. Richards never writes as a solipsist; he is merely making explicit what he has assumed: "out of these laws, these recurrent likenesses of behavior, IN OUR MINDS AND IN THE WORLD – not out of revived duplicates of individual past impressions – the fabric of our meaings, which is the world, is composed" (*PR*, page 36, my emphasis). This, says Richards, is the theorem upon which will be laid a new understanding of words.

A word, according to Richards, is "the missing parts of the contexts from which it draws its delegated efficacy ... when we mean the simplest-seeming concrete object, its concreteness comes to it from the way in which we are bringing it simultaneously into a number of sorts. The sorts grow together in it to form that meaning" (*PR*, page 35). Words have meaning only insofar as they have context. Context in-

---

[40] This distinction is developed by Ernst Cassirer in *Language and Myth*, trans. Susanne Langer (New York, 1946).

cludes not only the words printed or spoken on each side of a word, but also the situations of the producer and the perceiver of the word. Richards calls this contextual modification 'interinanimation'. The extension of this basic idea accounts for the seeming life of language. At the same time that the meaning of a word is being produced by a set of contexts, that same word-and-emerging-meaning is serving as a context for the words which mold it. This idea does not (as Richards seems to promise) solve the mystery of language, but it does prevent language from being treated as a series of inert bricks which can be piled into various shapes.

As usual, Richards is passionately sure that his current system is THE answer, but he admits that the contextual theory of interinanimation does not seem to apply to the language of science. The distinction is based upon that of *Science and Poetry*, but both the tone and diction are more palatable. He establishes a scale with poetic and scientific languages on opposite ends. The lack of interinanimation "is the ideal limit toward which we aim in exposition. Unfortunately we tend – increasingly since the 17th Century – to take rigid discourse as the norm, and impose its standards upon the rest of speech. This is much as if we thought that water, for all its virtues, in canals, baths and turbines, were really a weak form of ice."

The other end of the scale is in poetry – in some forms of poetry rather. We know very much less about the behavior of words in these cases – when their virtue is to have no fixed and settled meanings separable from those of the other words they occur with. There are many more possibilities here than the theory of language has yet tried to think out. Often the whole utterance in which the co-operating meanings of the component words hang on one another is not itself stable in meaning. It utters not one meaning but a movement among meanings. (*PR*, page 48)

The striking similarity of this hint at the way in which words mean and what we usually think of as the nature of metaphor makes it difficult not to label all language metaphor. But although all language is metaphorical, it does not follow that the relationships within the language must always produce a metaphor.[41] Although every word is

---

[41]   A number of critics maintain this position with variations. For example: Philip Wheelwright, *Metaphor and Reality*, suggests the metaphorical basis for such a seeming abstraction as the English verb *to be*. Sanskrit *asmi* (*I breathe*) yields *am* and *is*. The root *bhu* (*to grow*) yields *be*, and *vas* (*to dwell*) yields *was* (page 149). Walter J. Ong, "The Meaning of the 'New Criticism'", says "Metaphorical meaning is more tied to the material than meanings which are conventionally determined; it is fixed by a close dependence upon context, for if it becomes permanently

ultimately a metaphor for its referent, what we usually mean when we
say 'metaphor' is a compounded unit. In a sense, we mean the product
of the interinanimations of two meanings which are already the product
of interinanimation. Although every statement makes use of interinanimation, in the extreme case, metaphor, the interinanimations "will
go on moving as long as we bring fresh wits to study it. When Octavius
Caesar is gazing down at Cleopatra dead he says,

> She looks like sleep,
> As she would catch another Antony
> In her strong toil of grace.

. . . In what possible dictionary do the meanings of *toil* and *grace* come
to rest?" (*PR*, page 49). Here Richards is at last facing the unending
freshness of poetry. He who felt that psychology would at last make all
plain looks on Cleopatra through the eyes of Octavius and perceives
the limitation of man. From this point on, Richards insists that the
study of language is largely guesswork: the meanings of an utterance
"are resultants which we arrive at only through the interplay of the
interpretative possibilities of the whole utterance. In brief we have to
guess them . . .' (*PR*, page 55). But he insists that we must continue
to guess.

In *Principles of Literary Criticism* Richards asserted the importance
of irony, what he calls "the bringing in of the opposite, the complementary impulses" (page 250). In *The Philosophy of Rhetoric* the idea
is expanded and made more concrete. Now, his statements seem very
obvious; perhaps they were not so when he made them. Included in the
varieties of ways in which words are affected by elements which may
be irrational or fortuitous are all sorts of unexpected things: it may be
a shared phoneme, an overlapping of meaning, or it may even draw
meanings from "words, for example, which we might have used instead,
and, together with these, the reasons why we did not use them. Another
such extension looks to other uses, in other contexts, of what we, too

---

attached to a word, we no longer have metaphor" (p. 204). H. W. Wells, *Poetic
Imagery*, makes a distinction between 'the metaphorical comparison' and 'poetic
metaphor'. The first, he says, 'is purely descriptive', the second has 'a subjective
value' (p. 27). W. B. Stanford, *Greek Metaphor*, says, "Metaphor is the vital principle in all living languages. It is the verbal expression of the process and products
of the imagination with its powers of creative synthesis; it embodies in words what
the faculties of Association of Ideas and Thinking by Analogy produce in thoughts"
(p. 100). S. K. Langer, *Philosophy in a New Key*, affirms the ultimate metaphorical
quality of all language; she sees the 'fading' of metaphor as necessary to rapid
communication (p. 141).

simply, call 'the same word'" (*PR*, page 63). This suggests that a constant state of vigilance is necessary if the full meaning of a word in poetic context is to be perceived. It makes the reader a poet. Richards concentrates not on what the poet intends, but upon what the reader perceives. The two need not be the same. Readers of Donne and the Herberts do this, of course, and *Seven Types of Ambiguity*[42] is based almost entirely upon this principle. The value of the statement today is that it serves as a conscious reinforcement of what has become an almost instinctive practice.

But this line of speculation does suggest a face of metaphor, particularly important for the reading of Renaissance poetry, which is too often ignored. "The meaning of a word on some occasions is quite as much in what it keeps out, or at a distance, as in what it brings in" (*PR*, page 63). Petrarchan love poetry is the most obvious case, but the decadence of metaphysical poetry is also full of requests by the poet that the reader ignore all but a few of a word's possible meanings. This process is the obverse of decorum. It requires that the reader rigidly exclude, or mute, those possible points of comparison which detract from the direction intended by the poet. This presupposes an ability of the reader to know the poet's stance, helped by the 'attitude' and 'tone' of the poem. That this is often very difficult will be illustrated in Chapter Four, below. For convenience, a metaphor which achieves its primary effect as a result of the incongruities between its two halves may be called a 'negative metaphor', and a metaphor which requires a muting of incongruities may be called 'positive'.[43]

Richards does not perceive this distinction quite so clearly. In the broadest sense, of course, it does not exist. The principle of interinanimation can be extended to include everything so that a single word 'in context' includes not only all other words in the language, but all languages, and even all sounds. Communication, as he made clear in lecture one, is the process of divorcing elements small enough to convey a specific meaning, or area of meaning, from the totality of linguistic experience. Still, the distinction between positive and negative metaphors is implicit in Richards' work:

In philosophy, above all, we can take no step safely without an unrelaxing awareness of the metaphors we, and our audience, may be employing; and though we may pretend to eschew them, we can attempt to do so only by detecting them. And this is the more true, the more severe and abstract we

---

[42] William Empson, *Seven Types of Ambiguity* (London, 1930).
[43] These terms are developed in Chapter Four, A, below.

think the philosophy is . . . *The metaphors we are avoiding steer our thought as much as those we accept.* (*PR*, page 92, my emphasis)

From this it is but a step to discourse in which communication is achieved in part from what is not said, and to metaphor in which the basic incongruities are as important as the similarities.

At this stage Richards feels that he has achieved a basis from which a generalized definition of metaphor can be attempted. "In the simplest formulation, when we use a metaphor we have two thoughts of different things active together and supported by a single word, or phrase, whose meaning is a resultant of their interaction" (*PR*, page 93). This at first seems to be only the Johnsonian 'two ideas for one',[44] but Richards has actually suggested that it is one idea for two. Before the metaphor can exist (and so give two ideas for one), two ideas must first be combined to produce that unity. It is as though two threads were drawn through a single point and then separated again with each having been significantly changed by the drawing through the nexus with the other. The nature of the nexus is bewilderingly complex: "We find, of course, when we look closer that there is an immense variety in these modes of interaction between co-present thoughts . . . between different missing parts or aspects of the different contexts of a word's meaning" (*PR*, page 93). The internal-external nature of the perceptive act insists that each reading of a metaphor is to some extent unique. The wonder is that communication is ever possible. But as always, Richards is not cowed by the difficulties which he so clearly perceives:

Thought is metaphoric, and proceeds by comparison, and the metaphors of language derive therefrom. To improve the theory of metaphor we must remember this. And the method is to take more note of the skill in thought which we possess and are intermittently aware of already. We must translate more of our skill into discussable science. Reflect better upon what we do already so cleverly. Raise our implicit recognitions into explicit distinctions. (*PR*, pages 94-95)

The method, then, is to be inductive; the grounds for search are the mind as it perceives; and the tool is introspection.

[44] Although Samuel Johnson provides a convenient name upon which to hang theories of metaphor which make much of similarities, he was aware that in order to produce a 'simile' discrepancies are necessary. Wells quotes from the "Life of Addison": "A poetical simile is the discovery of likeness between two actions in general nature dissimilar, or of causes terminating by different operations in the same resemblance of effect. But the mention of another like consequence from a like cause, or of a like performance by a like agency, is not a simile but an exemplification" (Wells, p. 22).

It is to the production of such a method that Richards gives his attention in *The Philosophy of Rhetoric:*

A first step is to introduce two technical terms to assist us in distinguishing from one another . . . the two ideas that any metaphor, at its simplest, gives us. Let me call them the tenor and the vehicle . . . . For the whole task is to compare the different cases these two members of a metaphor hold to one another, and we are confused at the start if we do not know which of the two we are talking about. (*PR*, page 96)

'Tenor' is to designate "the underlying idea or principal subject which the vehicle or figure means" (page 97). The 'vehicle' is the figure which is brought in from outside the original context. 'Metaphor' is to be reserved for the double unit. The 'meaning' is the effect of the metaphor. 'Love' is tenor, 'rose' is vehicle, and 'love-rose' is metaphor. The meaning is the modification in love which has been achieved by making it co-present with rose.[45] Though these distinctions seem almost primitive, the avidity with which other critics have accepted them indicates the vacuum which they filled.

Once he has established a vocabulary which permits some analysis without total semantic confusion, Richards suggests an hypothesis:

---

[45] W. K. Wimsatt, Jr., *The Verbal Icon*, takes this line toward the relationships of tenor and vehicle. He recognizes the alteration in both which results from metaphor at its best. W. B. Stanford, *Greek Metaphor*, is Wimsatt's source: "The term metaphor is fully valid only when applied to a very definite and rather complicated concept, vis. the process and result of using a term (X) normally signifying an object or concept (A) in such a context that it must refer to another object or concept (B) which is distinct enough in characteristics from A to ensure that in the composite idea formed by the synthesis of the concepts A and B and now symbolized in the word X, the factors A and B retain their conceptual independence even while they merge in the unity symbolized by X; this integration of diversities is true metaphor; but on the other hand, if in the complex A B as symbolized by X either factor absorbs or over-shadows the other, then the metaphor is proportionally faulty and verges toward a trope like synechdoche or catachresis wherein there is no conscious concept of duality . . .; while secondly if the concepts or objects A and B are so incongruous that their composition fails to produce an integrated unity then the metaphor is either a failure or an enigma" (p. 101). Whalley, *Poetic Process*, says much the same: "I shall now maintain that metaphor is the means by which feelings can be fused without losing their individual clarity; that metaphor is the fundamental mode for transmuting feelings into words; that metaphor is the process by which the internal relationships peculiar to poetry are established . . . . But the influence of metaphor is not confined to illuminating only the terms it brings into collision. It can strike out a fresh image which cannot be produced in any more elementary way – an image which is not the sum of its elements nor their identity but one which grows to its individual form by a process of mutual enrichment, the elements of the metaphor cross-fertilizing each other" (pp. 141-146).

the copresence of the vehicle and tenor results in a meaning (to be clearly distinguished from the tenor) which is not attainable without their inter-action. That the vehicle is not normally a mere embellishment of a tenor which is otherwise unchanged by it but that vehicle and tenor in co-opera-tion give a meaning of more varied powers than can be ascribed to either. (*PR*, page 100)

If we add to this the idea that the combined tenor-vehicle, that is, the metaphor, yields a meaning greater and different than the sum of their two separate meanings, we have a practical explanation of Hulme's intensive manifold.

Richards next suggests a continuum upon which a metaphor may be placed to determine its nature. The relative importance of the tenor and vehicle to the meaning which the reader draws from the metaphor varies greatly. "At one extreme the vehicle may become almost a mere decoration or coloring of the tenor, at the other extreme, the tenor may become almost a mere excuse for the introduction of the vehicle" (*PR*, page 101). With this, Richards is ready for a practical discussion of metaphor, and for the first time in his work, his primary attention is upon metaphor, rather than upon some huge scheme. As any good rhetorician would, he begins by denying the value of those who hold views different from his. "The traditional discussion of metaphor is hardly more than a set of cautionary hints to over enthusiastic school-boys, hints masquerading as fundamental theory of language" (*PR*, page 103). He attributes this situation to the extremes of critical fail-ings: obtuseness and over-ingeniousness. The corrective for both is at hand:

First, that not to see how a word *can* work is never by itself sufficient proof that it will not work. Secondly, conversely, that to see how it ought to work will not prove that it does. Any detailed examination of metaphor brings us into such risk of pedantry and self-persuasion, that these morals seem worth stress. Yet a critical examination of metaphor, with these morals in mind, is

just now what literary criticism chiefly needs. (*PR*, page 106)
These warnings are to be kept in mind and another added to them. It is important to realize that the "exchanges between the meanings of words which we study in explicit verbal metaphors are superimposed upon a perceived world which is itself a product of earlier or unwitting metaphor, and we shall not deal with them justly if we forget that this is so" (*PR*, pages 108-109).

This is more than a reminder that all sorts of unexpected things are involved in reading a metaphor; it is the idea of 'negative metaphor' struggling for expression. In examining a passage from *Othello*,[46] he arrives at an almost conscious understanding: If the reader will analyze "interactions which do not work through *resemblances* between tenor and vehicle, but depend upon other relations between them including *disparities*, some of our most prevalent, over-simple, ruling assumptions about metaphors as comparisons are soon exposed" (*PR*, pages 107-108) .This is still polemic – the classical rhetorician at work – but as he nears the end of the final lecture, he restates the concept of negative metaphor (in all but name) clearly enough to warrant quoting at some length:

We must not, with the 18th Century, suppose that the interactions of tenor and vehicle are to be confined to their resemblances. There is disparity acting too. When Hamlet uses the word crawling, its force comes not only from whatever resemblances to vermin it brings in but at least equally from the differences that resist and control the influences of their resemblances. The implication there is that man should not so crawl. Thus, talk about the identification or fusion that a metaphor effects is nearly always misleading and pernicious. In general, there are very few metaphors in which disparities between tenor and vehicle are not as much operative as the similarities. Some similarity will commonly be the ostensive ground of the shift, but the peculiar modification of the tenor which the vehicle brings about is even more the work of their unlikenesses than of their likenesses. (*PR*, page 127)

Both negative and positive metaphors (a positive metaphor is one which operates upon similarities and demands a muting of contradictions) can be further analyzed in terms of a broad division based upon the nature of their grounds. As we might expect, one of these divisions is external, 'real', and the other internal, based upon particular sets of impulses. The first kind work "through some direct resemblance between the two things, the tenor and the vehicle". The second "work through some common attitude which we may (often through accidental and extraneous reasons) take up towards them both. The division is not final or irreducible, of course, *That we like them both* is, in one sense, a common property that two things share" (*PR*, page 118). This is true, but it is painful to watch Richards muddy the water which he has spent his career filtering. The division between stimulus and response is one of Richards' major accomplishments. Perhaps the suspension of this

[46]   Had it pleas'd heaven
To try me with affliction, had they rain'd
All kinds of sores, and shames, on my bare head,
Steep'd me in poverty to the very lips,
Given to captivity me and my utmost hopes . . . .
(Act IV, ii, 48-52)

division is simply the result of dealing with specific instances rather than abstract principles. In a particular metaphor it is as difficult to distinguish between internal and external elements of perception as it is to separate being and becoming in a particular work of art.

But, as Richards says, "It is better to make a mistake that can be exposed than to do nothing, better to have any account of how metaphor works . . . than to have none" (*PR*, page 115). In his comments on the polarity of vehicle and tenor ("Lecture Five"), Richards suggests a plan of attack upon the nature of metaphor. A careful investigator would set a spectrum labeling one extreme tenor and the other vehicle.[47] Once a sufficient number of examples had been so placed, the final step would be to examine the resultant groupings to see if the effect of a metaphor is to a significant degree determined by this particular emphasis. Perhaps the overwhelmingly subjective nature of the positioning deterred Richards, for he did not carry out the experiment. Possibly his student, William Empson, in *Seven Types of Ambiguity*, attempts such an experiment.

Instead, Richards makes a number of inductive leaps in what seems to be a premature attempt to arrive at general truths. The two most successful leaps are his comments upon the importance of negative metaphor and upon the obverse, dead, or wholly 'positive' metaphor. Enough has been said of the first, but his comments on positive metaphor are worth examining: In a sense such a metaphor has ceased to be a metaphor:

[If a figure of speech] carries not two ideas but only one . . . it has become 'adequated,' or is dead, and is no longer a metaphor. But however stone dead such metaphors seem, we can easily wake them up. (*PR*, page 101)

The most common way to awaken a dead metaphor is by setting it in an unusual or unexpected syntax.

There are two senses in which a metaphor may be thought of as carrying only one idea. Two ideas may be fused into a single new entity which is different from either of the parts, or the vehicle may be

---

[47] In complicated cases this positioning must be very difficult. For example: Ransom and Richards differ as to which is the tenor, which the vehicle in Denham's famous lines, "O could I flow like thee" (*The New Criticism*, p. 68). Wells, *Poetic Imagery*, makes a distinction between Direct and Inverse metaphor which is useful in this positioning. A Direct Metaphor is one in which the initial object suggests something beyond itself which is of primary importance. An inverse Metaphor occurs when the initial object suggests something beyond itself which reinforces the importance of the initial object (pp. 24-25). But of course there remains the problem of discovering which is the initial object.

muted progressively out of existence. In the first case the result is metaphor in the fullest sense. In the second the result is wholly un-metaphorical in the poetic sense. Hence, the 'leg' of a table and the 'back' of a truck. To awaken these moribund expressions it is necessary only to move the focus of attention from the tenor pole in the direction of the vehicle pole. To do so makes the reader once more aware of the incongruities which exist between tenor and vehicle, and the result is a live metaphor.

Richards' test for the life of a metaphor is deceptively simple. "If we cannot distinguish tenor from vehicle then we may provisionally take the word to be literal; if we can distinguish at least two cooperating uses, then we have metaphor" (*PR*, page 119). Richards, however, admits that "A word may be simultaneously both literal and meta-phoric" (*PR*, page 119). This is true because the distinction in difficult cases is subjective. The very attempt to decide whether or not a par-ticular example is a metaphor may well make the examiner conscious of metaphorical relationships of which neither he nor the poet was aware. This would seem to be an extra dividend (or danger) of poetic analysis. There are occasions upon which Richards seems to take words for things, or to impute 'life' to the word itself rather than to the mind which perceives it, but on the whole his criticism is remarkably free of objective-subjective confusion.

Before examining the modifications which later critics have made in Richards' systems, two warnings which Richards issues must be noted. The first is a suggestion for a further clarification of the vocabulary of metaphorical analysis. Just as it is essential that the differences among tenor, vehicle, and metaphor be kept clearly in mind, so too there must be a distinction between tenor and meaning. The danger is "the mis-taking of what I have been calling the tenor-vehicle antithesis for that between the metaphor (the double unity including tenor and vehicle) and its meaning. These two antitheses are easy to confuse . . ." (*PR*, page 132). The distinction is more difficult than at first appears. It may be stated in this fashion. A metaphor is composed of idea (tenor) and idea (vehicle). Both ideas are embodied in images. The tenor about which the poet is primarily speaking – that which is a continuation of his general discourse – is a meaning which in other circumstances could function as vehicle for some other tenor. Without implying a value judgment, we may say that the vehicle is a secondary 'meaning' which is used to alter the fundamental meaning in a particular direction. It is possible, of course, to have a pair of complementary metaphors in which roles are reversed. My love is a horse, and My horse is my love. But whichever function is designated by the context as tenor, there is another relationship which must be kept distinct in analysis. Once the tenor and vehicle have combined to produce a single, new thing, this new thing bears a particular relationship to the larger meaning which the poet is expressing. The modification which the metaphor makes upon the larger unit of meaning is the meaning of the metaphor.

The metaphor (itself made up of a combined tenor and vehicle) may be used as a vehicle for a larger tenor, the next wider unity of meaning – and so on. A poem is thus a series of intensive manifolds which may be analyzed as though they were extensive so long as it is realized that such an analysis does not account for the poem, but only describes a part of its existence. Richards' principle of 'Interinanimation' suggests not only a mutual altering of a word and those words which make up the context into which it grows, but also that the product of this initial interinanimation is itself immediately subject to further alteration as a result of the larger context into which it inevitably is placed.

Richards' first caution is directed largely at critics; his second warning is for poets and readers. The realization of the possibilities of negative metaphor provide a great temptation: "The opposed conception of comparison – as a mere putting together of two things to see what will happen – is a contemporary fashionable aberration, which takes an extreme case as the norm" (*PR*, page 123). This particular fashion "is the opposite position from Johnson's, for whereas Johnson objected to comparisons being, like Cowley's, 'far fetched', it is the distance of the fetching here which is the merit" (*PR*, page 124). The value of this far-fetching, though, in spite of the danger, is not to be denied:

As the two things put together are more remote, the tension created is, of course, greater. That tension is the spring of the bow, the source of the energy of the shot, but we ought not to mistake the strength of the bow for the excellence of the shooting; or the strain for the aim. And bafflement is an experience of which we soon tire, and rightly. But as we know, what seems an impossible connection, an 'impracticable identification,' can at once turn into an easy and powerful adjustment if the right hint comes from the rest of the discourse. (*PR*, page 126)

The poet, then, has the obligation to include the 'right hint' within the poem; otherwise, he misses the target. A major function of the 'close-reading' critic is to discover this 'right hint' and explain it to the reader. So long as the critic gets the hint from the artifact, all is well, but if he draws it instead from a personal association, it becomes very difficult to determine whether the critic is acute and the reader dull, or the reader sensible and the critic over ingenious.

In the last lecture of *The Philosophy of Rhetoric*, Richards quarrels with T. E. Hulme, his predecessor, and praises William Empson, his successor. Despite the vehemence of his attack upon Hulme, as we have seen, the two have much in common. And Richards must at least credit Hulme for saying something, rather than nothing, about the nature of metaphor. The praise for Empson is based upon his ability to supply the 'right hint from the rest of the discourse':

Let us consider more closely what happens in the mind when we put together – in a sudden and striking fashion – two things belonging to very different orders of experience. The most important happenings – in addition to a general confused reverberation and strain – are the mind's efforts to connect them. The mind ... works only by connecting, and it can connect any two things in an indefinitely large number of different ways. Which of these it chooses is settled by reference to some larger whole or aim, and, though we may not discover its aim, the mind is never aimless. In all interpretation we are filling in connections, and for poetry, of course, our freedom to fill in – the absence of explicitly stated intermediate steps – is the main source of its power. (*PR*, pages 124-125)

It is satisfying to see Richards asserting in clear form the same principles which he had groped for in *The Foundations of Aesthetics*. The principal differences are of language – the metaphors he chooses – not in meaning.[48]

[48]   Ransom, *The World's Body*, does not see this unity (p. 155).

II

THE SECOND GENERATION: WILLIAM EMPSON, ALLEN TATE, JOHN CROWE RANSOM, CLEANTH BROOKS

> — so far as poetry can be regarded altogether dispas-
> sionately, so far as it is an external object for examina-
> tion, it is dead poetry and not worth examining; fur-
> ther, so far as a critic has made himself dispassionate
> about it, so far as he has repressed sympathy in favour
> of curiosity, he has made himself incapable of examin-
> ing it.
>
> *Seven Types of Ambiguity*

A. THE ATTITUDE OF WILLIAM EMPSON[1]

William Empson is at once the most brilliant and the least theoretical of the critics who followed, and reacted against, the principles set forth by I. A. Richards. He consciously blurs the distinction between poet and reader that Richards is at such pains to establish. Such a distinction, he says, "might be more tidy, but ... it would itself claim too much; the rules as to what is conveyable are so much more mysterious even than the rules governing the effects of ambiguity ... that it is better to talk about both parties at once, and be thankful if what you say is true about either" (page 274). Empson is very aware of the limitation imposed by the fallacy of subjective statistic, but he, like Richards, feels that any analysis is better than none:

I must confess I find the crudity and latent fallacy of a psychologist dis-
cussing verses that he does not enjoy less disagreeable than the blurred and
tasteless refusal to make statements of an aesthete who conceives himself to
be only interested in Taste. (page 15)

His critical method, which he says must 'seem very dubious', is to produce a "possible set of alternative meanings with some ingenuity", and then to say that the meaning "is grasped in the preconsciousness of

[1] William Empson, *Seven Types of Ambiguity*, 3rd ed. (New York, 1955). First published (London, 1930). All future page references will be included in the text.

the reader by a native effort of the mind" (page 270). And for those critics who find him wanting, as it is easy to do, in specific statements about poems which fall within their specialty, he has a perfect, and perfectly opaque, answer: "many of my explanations may be demonstrably wrong, and yet efficient for their purpose, and *vice versa*" (page 286). What then, is his purpose in establishing types?

Thus I think my seven types form an immediately useful set of distinctions, but to a more serious analysis they would appear trivial and hardly to be distinguished from one another. I call them useful, not merely as a means of stringing examples, but because, in complicated matters, any distinction between cases, however irrelevant, may serve to heighten one's consciousness of the cases themselves. (page 286)

Altogether, it is easy to see that Empson has not a system, but an attitude. His goal is to demonstrate the value of an open and vigilant mind drawing upon the resources of wide and varied experiences to a proper reading of poetry. He is not, however, a mere impressionist, but rather a close reader who has considerable powers of introspection. For him, reading is an art.

We may note Empson's conception of the critic and his function and method before proceeding to the business of metaphor. The position of a literary critic is far more social than scientific, he says, and there is no possibility of finishing the criticism of any single work, for "so far as people are always reading an author, he is always being read differently. It is the business of the critic to extract for his public what it wants; to organise, what he may indeed create, the taste of his period."[2] The qualifications of such critics in our time are rigorous. "They must possess a fair amount of equilibrium or fairly strong defences; they must have the power first of reacting to a poem sensitively, and definitely:

and then, having fixed the reaction . . . they must be able to turn the microscope on it with a certain indifference and without smudging it with their fingers . . . and have enough detachment not to mind what their sources of satisfaction may turn out to be. (page 279)

Empson cheerfully faces the untenable position of the critic, realizing that it is really no more difficult than the position of poetry.

Empson does not concern himself primarily with the function of metaphor. He is rather interested in a larger aspect of poetry which he

[2] Empson's attitude is similar to the attitudes of Arnold, Eliot, and Tate, though Empson does not suggest that poetry should take the place of religion, nor that it is primarily the man of letters upon whose shoulders rests culture.

calls 'ambiguity'. The relationship between ambiguity and metaphor is not a simple one. Almost all metaphors are, by Empson's definition, ambiguous to some extent, but there are many sorts of ambiguity which are not metaphors. By 'ambiguity' Empson does not mean quite what common usage suggests:

An ambiguity, in ordinary speech, means something very pronounced, and as a rule witty or deceitful. I propose to use the word in an extended sense, and shall think relevant to my subject any verbal nuance, however slight, which gives room for alternative reactions to the same piece of language. (page 3)

From this definition it would appear that ambiguity is involved in all language except the Ricardian language of science, for there is always 'room for alternative reactions' no matter how specific the writer may have intended to be. This first attempt at definition presupposes Richards' theories of perception, and shows remarkable affinity to Cassirerian thought. It suggests that ambiguity does not reside in syntax or diction, but in the mind of the reader, in his 'reactions'. But Empson sees no need to maintain the distinction between stimulus and response and suggests a 'prudent man' criterion for establishing the degree and kind of ambiguity:

We call it ambiguous, I think, when we recognise that there could be a puzzle as to what the author meant, in that alternative views might be taken without sheer misreading. If a pun is quite obvious it would not ordinarily be called ambiguous, because there is no room for puzzling. But if an irony is calculated to deceive a section of its readers I think it would ordinarily be called ambiguous, even by a critic who has never doubted its meaning. No doubt one could say that even the most obvious irony is a sort of playing at deception, but it may imply that only a comic butt could be deceived, and this makes a different sort of irony . . . . Thus the criterion for the ordinary use of the word is that somebody might be puzzled, even if not yourself. (pages x-xi)

This definition is still far from 'plurisignification'; it suggests that the 'puzzlement' as to which of several meanings is intended may be solved, and gives the critic license to know the intent of the author and the degree of comprehension of the 'average' reader. In the terms to be developed in Chapter Five, B, he is appealing to cultural norms. Without considerably more theoretical basis than he provides "This must be very dubious." Empson suggests that for the critic of good taste, rigorous theoretical principles are at best useful fictions and at worst irrelevant pedanticisms. In his confidence in 'taste' he resists the division of critical effort which Frye makes between the study of criticism and the study of literature.

He does much better in his earlier attempts at definition of ambiguity:

The fundamental situation, whether it deserves to be called ambiguous or not, is that a word or a grammatical structure is effective in several ways at once. (page 5)

The key word here is 'effective'; ambiguity as here defined must be the principal device of a poetry of inclusion. When he speaks of the function of ambiguity, his kinship to Richards is very clear. "The device is used ... to give an interpenetrating, and, as it were, fluid unity, in which phrases will go either with the sentence before or after and there is no break in the movement of the thought" (page 60). This last definition, which is concerned with syntax and hence is easier to illustrate than ambiguity of diction, suggests that 'the movement of thought' – the tenor – must incorporate alternative meanings. This is parallel to Richards' definition of metaphor, but the term 'ambiguity', Empson admits, is still hazy:

I do not deny that the term had better be used as clearly as possible, and that there is a use for a separate term "double meaning," for example when a pun is not felt to be ambiguous in effect. But it could be argued that, until you have done your analysis of ambiguities, you cannot be sure whether the total effect is ambiguous or not; and that this forces you in some degree to extend the meaning of the term. (page xii)

This returns almost to the starting point; all possible constructions are in some degree, at some time, and to someone, ambiguous. If this is so, how is one to operate critically with a term which represents the universal situation and is definable only subjectively? Empson tells us how to avoid the problem:

The conservative attitude to ambiguity is curious and no doubt wise; it allows a structure of associated meanings to be shown in a note, but not to be admitted; the reader is encouraged to swallow the thing by a decent reserve; it is thought best not to let him know that he is thinking in such complicated terms. So it is assumed ... that Shakespeare can only have meant one thing, but that the reader must hold in mind a variety of things he may have meant, and weigh them, in appreciating the poetry, according to their probabilities.... Very likely the editors do not seriously believe their assumption; indeed I have myself usually said "either ... or" when meaning "both ... and." (page 94)

Here, most clearly, is expressed the attitude of William Empson; if it works, do it, and never mind the theories of aesthetics, semantics, or ontology.

This cavalier attitude makes Empson's system perhaps not worth mastering,[3] but it makes him very aware of the complexity of the perceptive act as well as the dangers of too confident statements about that act:

There are three possible scales or dimensions, that seem of reliable importance, along which ambiguities may be spread out: the degree of logical or grammatical disorder, the degree to which the apprehension of the ambiguity must be conscious, and the degree of psychological complexity concerned. Of these the first seems the one about which there is least danger of

[3] I here set down Empson's definitions as given in the analytical table of contents to *Seven Types* and J. C. Ransom's definitions of Empson's seven types which are presented in *The New Criticism*. It is at once obvious that theoretical confusion is impossible to avoid. Although Empson admits to that confusion, admission does not substantially reduce anarchy.

   I. Empson: "First-type ambiguities arise when a detail is effective in several ways at once, e.g. by comparisons with several points of likeness, antitheses with several points of difference, 'comparative' adjectives, subdued metaphors, and extra meanings suggested by rhythm."

      Ransom: "Where one thing is likened to another, and by virtue not of one resemblance but of more than one."

  II. Empson: "In second-type ambiguities two or more alternative meanings are fully resolved into one."

      Ransom: "Where one locution has two or more meanings, but they take the same logical direction."

 III. Empson: "The condition for third-type ambiguity is that two apparently unconnected meanings are given simultaneously."

      Ransom: "Where one locution simultaneously has two meanings, and only one of them has logical relevance. This type includes pun."

 IV. Empson: "In the fourth type the alternative meanings combine to make clear a complicated state of mind in the author."

      Ransom: "Where one locution has two or more meanings which do not agree very well."

  V. Empson: "The fifth type is a fortunate confusion, as when the author is discovering his idea in the act of writing ... or not holding it all in mind at once."

      Ransom: "Where the poet decides upon his meaning in the middle of a passage, so that the beginning and the end of the passage will not be relevant to each other."

 VI. Empson: "In the sixth type what is said is contradictory or irrelevant and the reader is forced to invent interpretations."

      Ransom: "Where the logical reader is obliged to paraphrase a locution into conflicting statements, though the poet does not make them."

VII. Empson: "The seventh type is that of full contradiction, marking a division in the author's mind."

      Ransom: "Where one locution has two meanings which are plainly in opposition."

talking nonsense, the one to which least critical attention has so far been paid. My seven types, so far as they are not merely a convenient framework, are intended as stages of advancing logical disorder. However, I shall continually have to be using the other two criteria, and the three are not wholly independent of one another . . . . (page 57)

The first of these three, the sense in which ambiguity can to some degree be assigned to the structure of the poem, rather than to the poet or the reader, is the one which appeals to Ransom and to a lesser extent to Brooks. But in practice, Empson, Ransom, and Brooks, all three, concentrate on the degree of psychological complexity. It may be that logical and grammatical disorder is simply the vehicle for presenting psychological complexity, and hence the ultimate task of criticism is to explore either the mind of the poet in creation or the mind of the reader in perception, though of course the inception and goal of that study must be the artifact.

Such theory of perception as Empson sets forth is taken from I. A. Richards; the basic unit of poetry is for Empson, as for Richards, the engram. Though he does not attempt lists of the co-efficients of reader response, the neurological chart in *Principles of Literary Criticism* is not an unfair presentation of Empson's ideas of perception:

It is these faint and separate judgments of probability which unite, as if with an explosion to "make sense" and accept the main meaning of a connection of phrases; and the reaction, though rapid, is not as immediate as one is liable to believe. Also as in a chemical reaction, there will have been reverse or subsidiary reaction, or small damped explosions, or slow widespread reaction, not giving out much heat, going on concurrently, and the final result may be complicated by preliminary stages in the main process, or after-effects from the products of the reaction. (page 21)

Despite the Ricardian tone of this metaphor, there is, in Empson, a substantial difference in emphasis. Empson gives a good deal more credit to the volitional powers of the reader's mind than does Richards. 'Judgment' is a term which only rarely occurs in Richards' systems. Then too, Empson never loses sight of the fact that his chemical description of perception is a metaphor, and so he is not betrayed into a too mechanical description of the process of reading. The basic difference between the two men is that whereas Richards wishes to understand the process of perception step by step, Empson is often content to see the results and not worry about how, exactly, they were achieved. By this I do not mean that Empson leaps to conclusions, but rather that his method is to proceed by illustration rather than theory. There is thus no built-in protection against over-ingenuity or dullness; common sense is the only safeguard. Empson teaches this in the only way that it can be taught, by example.

Although it is impossible to arrive at a single conception of ambiguity according to Empson, something can be gained by following his example – by looking to illustrations and results rather than to theoretical distinctions:

The way in which opposites can be stated so as to satisfy a wide variety of people, for a great number of degrees of interpretation, is the most important thing about the communication of the arts. (page 249)

Here, without so much as a mention of 'ambiguity', Empson gives a workable sense of what he is after. Had he considered it worth his while, he might have presented the philosophical assumptions behind this statement in some manner such as this: "Since the world is made up of a balance of opposites, since man himself is constantly balanced among numberless contending impulses, and since a single perception gains its quality by virtue of its specific place on a continuum between opposites, the tool which best enables man to discern his station and function at any single moment within the flux must necessarily itself be a complex of potentially contradictory elements and must also support contradictory perceptions within a single individual – must make provision for a multiplicity of individual interpretations which result from the contradictory backgrounds of various readers." "And *vice versa*", Empson would probably add. Still, this seems to be what he means by 'meaningful ambiguity', and the vitality of the contradiction noted combined with the degree to which the poet/reader has come to terms with the discrepancy is the basis for the division of ambiguity.

Since the nature of opposites – their conflicts and resolutions – is Empson's most significant addition to Richards' ideas on metaphor, it is necessary to quote Empson at length:

one might say . . . that the idea of "opposite" is a comparatively late human invention, admits of great variety of interpretation (having been introduced wherever there was an intellectual difficulty), and corresponds to nothing in the real world; that $-a \cdot b$ is contrary to a for all values of b; that words in poetry, like words in primitive languages (and like, say, the Latin *altus*, high or deep, the English *let*, allow or hinder), often state a pair of opposites without any overt ambiguity; that in such a pair you are only stating, for instance a scale, which might be extended between any two points, though no two points are in themselves opposites; and that in searching for greater accuracy one might say "2 per cent. white" and mean a very black shade of grey. Or one might admit that the criterion in this last type becomes psychological rather than logical, in that the crucial point of definition has become the idea of context, and the total attitude to that context of the individual. A contradiction of this kind may be meaningless, but can never be blank; it has at least stated the subject which is under discussion, and has given a sort of intensity to it such as one finds in a gridiron pattern in architecture because it gives prominence neither to the horizontals nor the verticals . . . . so that whatever tendencies to action are aroused . . . there is just the same claim being made on the other side, and one is drawn taut between the two similar impulses into the stasis of appreciation. (pages 217-218)

This passage might well serve as a link between Richards and Tate. Empson here shows that a poetry of inclusion is quite the same as a poetry of tension. The criterion for both must be psychological. "Altus" and "let" are puns, though most often they are not so felt. And since puns are the most obvious of verbal ambiguities, it is to their nature that Empson directs his attention. "To say a thing in two parts is different in incalculable ways from saying it as a unit; Coleridge says somewhere that the mind insists on having a single word for a single mental operation, and will use an inadequate word rather than two adequate ones" (page 259). The most obvious way to do this is to pun, but for a pun to present a meaningful ambiguity, both meanings of the word must be applicable to the same context, and the meanings must differ sufficiently so that one is not merely an illustration of the other.

The relationship between pun and metaphor is puzzling. A metaphor gives one thing for two; a pun (in either spelling or pronunciation, or in both) gives two things for one. Metaphors are necessary because, "When you are holding a variety of things in your mind, or using for a single matter a variety of intellectual machinery, the only way of applying all our criteria is to apply them simultaneously . . . the only way of not giving something heterogeneous is to give something which is at every point a compound" (page 269).[4] Puns most often seem to have their source in accident. Metaphors and puns both achieve their effects by a telescoping syntax. The relationships among 'ambiguity', 'metaphor', and 'pun' are suggested in the three intersecting circles, circles which are constructed as a visual aid, not as a complete representation of the incredibly complicated verbal activity which they only can serve to indicate.

[4] This, perhaps, accounts for Empson's almost perverse refusal to narrow the meaning of 'ambiguity'. Its plurisignificative nature is a virtue, allowing the critic to refer to a number of things at the same time while yet limiting, in some degree, the quality about which he speaks.

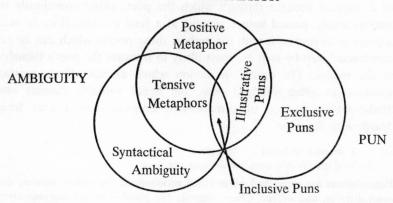

It may be well to review the terms employed here. 'Meaningful Ambiguity' is the simultaneous presence of two possible interpretations which enable the perceiver to make better sense of life's paradoxes than he would otherwise be able to do. 'Metaphor' is the juxtaposition of two ideas, images, or emotions which combine to produce a third entity which can be expressed in no other way. 'Pun' refers to a word (either sight or sound) which may suggest two quite different meanings to one who perceives it. Both meanings must be suggested by the syntax, though it is not necessary that they be relevant to the same syntax. A syntactical or logical ambiguity depends on verbal elements larger than a word. A metaphor of tension makes use of oppositions between tenor and vehicle, as well as similarities. Positive metaphor concentrates on similarities between tenor and vehicle. An exclusive pun does not make its two meanings relevant to the same syntax. In an illustrative pun, one meaning serves as analogy to the other; since the concentration is upon the similarities between the two meanings and both are relevant to the same syntax, it is also a metaphor of the positive kind. An inclusive pun is a metaphor of tension because both meanings are relevant to the same context and the oppositions between the two function to produce the effect upon the perceiver. Puns, of course, are felt to be puns only in context; therefore, no word taken by itself can be a metaphor. It is only when context (including the psychological context of the reader) brings both meanings to mind at once that puns can be either ambiguous or metaphorical.

Empson says that 'Inclusive Puns' are more common than one would suppose. Though he disapproves of poets who depend upon puns (page 101), he nevertheless sees what he calls the 'subdued pun' as a basic technique in poetic composition. A subdued pun is the vestige of a stage of thought through which the poet, either consciously or unconsciously, passed before arriving at a final version. Since to read a poem is to rewrite it with the author, those poems which can be reconstructed step-by-step are most likely to transmit the poet's thoughts to the reader. The cruces in diction which exercise Shakespearian scholars are often subdued puns and hence valuable insights into Shakespeare's method of composition. Empson uses a crux from *Macbeth* to illustrate:

> I am sick at heart . . . this push
> Will cheere me ever, or dis-eate me now.

Emendations are *chair* and *cheer* (then pronounced the same); *disseat, disease, disseize*, and *defeat. Cheer* suggests the plaudits of a victorious army and recovery from melancholia; *eate* suggests the hostile army, regarded as an ogre that would eat him up, and the remorse that was gnawing at his entrails. (page 96)

Empson notes the usual method of explaining away a crux in diction: scribal error, baffled printer, false memory – and then suggests that the confusion may have been Shakespeare's intent: "you may say that Shakespeare actually intended, by putting down something a little removed from any of the approximate homonyms, to send the reader groping about their network" (pages 96-97). This is the intentional fallacy with a vengeance, but whatever may be the case in terms of Shakespeare's intent, it is good advice for the reader. Since a subdued pun may be tied to neither one definition nor the other, and yet may contain something of both, producing a third meaning, it is a metaphor. How is one to distinguish such pun-metaphors? "It is important to bear in mind this attitude to grammar; once these floating and ill-attached parts of speech are crushed together into a pun . . . it is a matter, not of calculation, but of experiment, to see what corrections to the formula must be applied" (page 235).

The overt (exclusive) pun is a lesser mode of aesthetic expression. Since the poet has ruled out many of the possible meanings, the reader can achieve at best a limited balance among the possible opposing forces suggested by the ambience of a word. The best overt puns are those which preserve something of the force of dramatic irony:

> Ye, who appointed stand
> Do as you have in charge, and briefly touch
> What we propound, and loud that all may hear.
>   (*Paradise Lost*, VI, 565 ff)

In an overt pun, the main thing to be noted is the cleverness of the poet in seeing that two words, though alike, mean very different things. Of course the passage from *Paradise Lost* is more complex than Empson notes. The speaker is a fallen angel who is illustrating his character by the superficiality of his wit. And the speech-gunpowder pun is a skillful illustration of the effect of Lucifer's rash words. Empson goes to verse which does not qualify as poetry in order to find pure puns of exclusion. His definition of the highest poetry as a means of presenting the contradictory unity of experience rules out the simple overt pun as a satisfactory device.

A final example from Empson's discussion of puns provides an implicit definition of metaphor. The lines are from Johnson's "London":

> With warbling eunuchs fill a licensed stage
> And lull to servitude a thoughtless age.

... this, I take it, is a joke, one would say it with an accent on *licensed* and look knowingly at the listener to make sure he saw the point. You may say this is only the use of a technical word in a generalised sense, but it is not a metaphor; the two meanings are different and he means to say both of them. (pages 123-124)

One might have expected Empson to have perceived or invented some way of unifying the two meanings of licensed, by etymology most obviously, or by some system such as Blake's Urizen, but of course the sympathetic reader of *Seven Types* has learned to do this for himself. What is significant here is the distinction between pun and metaphor. A pun is a single thing which gives 'two things for one'. A metaphor, apparently, is a single thing made of two, 'one thing for two'. This distinction is familiar, but in practical terms it does not always hold: in the frequent *sun-Son* pun/metaphor, the device is not purely a pun because the grounds for identification are so many and so strong that a metaphor results, and yet at the same time it is not strictly a metaphor because the "two meanings are different and he means to say both of them". This peculiar middle ground is the normal realm of allegory (in which the entire structure is a metaphor); it is the root of religious symbolism, and may generally be classed as a pun of illustration, though a sense of 'icon' may make such puns inclusive.

The notion that, at its extreme, metaphor is a reconciliation of opposites causes Empson to speculate in theory for an unusually long time. The idea of Freudian opposites gives the reader-as-poet a powerful tool for building a poem, though it may often lead him to the 'wrong' poem:

Now a Freudian opposite at least marks dissatisfaction; the notion of what you want involves the idea that you have not got it, and this again involves the "opposite defined in your context," which is what you have and cannot avoid. In more serious cases, causing wider emotional reverberations, such as are likely to be reflected in language, in poetry, or in dreams, it marks a centre of conflict; the notion of what you want involves the notion that you must not take it, and this again involves the "opposite defined by your context," that you want something different in another part of your mind. Of course conflict need not be expressed overtly as contradiction, but it is likely that those theories of aesthetics which regard poetry as the resolution of a conflict will find their illustrations chiefly in the limited field covered by the seventh type. (pages 218-219)

Empson realizes that 'the resolution of a conflict' is only one of the modes of poetry, but the effect of his book is to make such tensive poetry seem the best kind. It is to this device that *Seven Types* builds. In its baldest form the employment of Freudian opposites by a reader is destructive: "My point is not so much that these two are mixed up as that the poet has shown precisely by insisting that they were *the same*, that he knew they were distinguishable" (page 169). This suggests that whether the poet knows it or not he means the opposite of what he says. Empson's good taste saves him from the enormities which this implies, and of course he is not prepared to so yield the poet's position to the libido. Words which unite opposites "are seldom or never actually formed in a language to express the conflict between them; such words come to exist for more sensible reasons, and may then be used to express conflict.... In so far ... as you know that two things are opposites, you know a relation between them" (page 221). Such a theory allows Empson to have it both ways. Taste is the only guide.

In his discussion of Hopkins' "The Windhover", Empson makes explicit the claim of excellence for this "Freudian use of opposites, where two things thought of as incompatible, but desired intensely by different systems of judgments, are spoken of simultaneously by words applying to both; both desires are thus given a transient and exhausting satisfaction, and the two systems of judgment are forced into open conflict before the reader" (page 255). Empson's evaluation of the effects of this process show very clearly that this ultimate ambiguity is at the root of the most intense aesthetic communication. These Freudian opposites, "one might imagine, could pierce to regions that underlie the whole structure of our thought; could tap the energies of the very depths of the mind" (page 255).

This is very like Richards' assertion that metaphor is a suitable vehicle for expressing the modes of the 'depths of the mind', for a metaphor contains the seeds of the neurological activity which results in a balance of impulses. Although he deals with metaphor well, Empson's direct theoretical statements as to its nature are conventional. "One thing is said to be like another, and they have several different properities in virtue of which they are alike" (page 5). He makes a distinction between fused and nonfused metaphors which is reminiscent of Hulme's distinction between fancy and metaphor, between intensive and extensive manifolds. If an unfused metaphor occurs, the poet has not seen the essential unity of his materials:

he satisfies two opposite impulses, and as a sort of apology, admits that they contradict, but claims that they are like the soluble contradictions, and can safely be indulged .... he claims the sympathy of his audience in that "we can none of us say more than this," and gains dignity in that even from the poor material of human ignorance he can distil grace of style. (page 223)

It is obvious that Empson prefers another method of creation; the tone is derisive, yet he can see the practical justification of "feeling and not knowing one's way about the matter in hand". It would at first appear, he says, that such poems must be foolish in that "even if they say anything to one who understands them, [they] can quite justifiably say the opposite to one who does not". But again Empson does not say that such poetry is without value, for even if the poet has not succeeded in fusing his materials into a single unit, a metaphor, it is possible for the reader to do so, because "any contradiction is likely to have some sensible interpretations; and if you think of interpretations which are not sensible, it puts the blame on you" (page 223). Richards' warnings of the futility of ambiguity without direction need to be borne in mind here, and Empson's comments on Shelley indicate that not all contradictions are useful (page 181).

But even when Empson is sure that the poet did not know what he spoke of, it may happen that a 'fortunate muddle' will produce a telescoping of comparisons which fuse: "Shakespeare's *Ariachne* (*Troilus* V. 4), for Arachne and Ariadne, those two employers of thread, is a shining example" (page 182). The same sort of action, but this time intentional rather than fortunate, is granted a haiku:

Swiftly the years, beyond recall.
Solemn the stillness of this spring morning.
... lacking rhyme, metre, and any overt device such as comparison, these

lines are what we should normally call poetry only by virtue of their com-
pactness; two statements are made as if they were connected, and the reader
is forced to consider their relations for himself; the reason why those facts
should have been selected for a poem is left for him to invent; he will invent
a variety of reasons and order them in his own mind. This I think, is the
essential fact about the poetical use of language. (page 30)

This is an extreme case. The poet has produced an artifact which does
not contain the 'right hint' from which the reader can produce a fusion.
The seeds of Richards' 'neurological balance' are not in the lines. The
reader, if he is to experience a fusion, must do so almost completely on
his own. If a poem is the combination which results from the engrams
called up by the stimuli of the artifact, the reader is in a very important
sense creating a poem in the reading of his haiku. In this particular
case, any resolution which is achieved seems to me to be forced. The
goal is acceptance rather than fusion, and quite often such acceptance
is the aim of haiku.[5] Acceptance does not demand the fusion which
Hulme, Richards, and Empson see as the major power of metaphor.
And yet the lines may have a very powerful effect.

So far Empson's ideas have been discussed in relation to what I call
'negative' metaphor which gains its force from the disparity of its
elements – the distance between tenor and vehicle. But Empson is aware
of the existence and utility of 'positive' metaphor, metaphor which
insists on a nearly one-to-one relationship between tenor and vehicle.
For communication to succeed a great many things must be present in
the mind at the same time, but:

A complementary sort of implication may be defined: what must *not* be in
mind if the sentence is to be suitable, what it leaves vague, or is not thinking
about, or does not feel. The negative here assumes you might expect this
particular thing to be in mind, because otherwise you would not have
thought of it as an implication. You might think it lessened the importance
of a negative implication that one is only conscious of it if its assumption is
unjustified; but the mind is a destroyer; any assumption may chance to be
questioned; and most people are conscious that they, therefore, can to some
extent impose what they assume. (page 35)

The implications of this for negative metaphor are obvious. A poet's
meaning may be conveyed by what he chooses not to say; he may relate
two things by placing them in a single metaphor when he means to
indicate that they are totally different. This is a basic device of verbal
irony and of parody. As is often the case, all that keeps this Empsonian
system from total chaos is good sense.

[5]   This acceptance is what John Crowe Ransom calls 'Heterogeneity'.

So much for the negative; but since communication is possible, how does 'good sense' achieve it? If the reader is to construct his reactions to a poem from materials presented in the artifact, and if the materials may seem to mean the opposite of what they say, how is he to achieve an engrammatic complex which has anything at all in common with that the poet had in mind when he assembled the materials for the artifact? That, says Empson, is a difficult question. He chooses the dead metaphor as the best case in point:

... English is perhaps uniquely full of metaphors of this sort, which are not dead but sleeping, and, while making a direct statement, colour it with an implied comparison .... they are harder to use than either plain word or metaphor because if you mix them you must show you are conscious of their meaning, and are not merely being insensitive to the possibilities of the language. (pages 30-31)

This places the responsibility back on the poet, but since all language is basically metaphorical, any statement is filled with 'mixed metaphor' if all the possible metaphors are awake. This would seem to make communication impossible. Yet poets and readers communicate well enough to be aware of degrees of communication. This is true, Empson says, because in getting to know a piece of writing, we learn first of all which of the possible meanings of a word or syntactical pattern must be left out. A convenient term for this paring down of the body of meaning which surrounds a word is 'muting'. We mute unwanted elements so well, says Empson, that "we are actually surprised when they are brought out by a parody" (p. xiv).

In addition to the interinanimations which Richards suggests as the mode of this muting and which are, perhaps, a more satisfactory explanation than Empson's, Empson says that the fashion of a literary period may provide a signal for muting or not muting. The extreme cases are seventeenth-century baroque and eighteenth-century neo-classical:

The grotesque seventeenth-century simile ... belongs to an age of collections of interesting oddities rather than to the scientific age, with its limitations as to what is likely to be true and what it is sensible to say; to an age when all kinds of private fancies were avowable in their own rights. (page 250)

This is, in effect, a justification of historical criticism. If one is to read a poem correctly, he must be able to reconstruct the milieu in which it was written. Here we have a denial of pure impressionism and even perhaps of poetry as *sub specie aeternitatis*. It seems to me that Empson has put the case so strongly as to partially contradict himself. Whatever the age in which a poem is read, it "is the business of the reader to extract the meanings useful to him and ignore the meanings he thinks foolish" (page 223). Here Empson returns the power to the reader. Still, his point is valid. In seventeenth century poetry, "because its taste seems to have been curiously free from such critical principles as interpose a judgment before the experience of accepting the poetry is completed", we must read for ambiguities. But if we search for the same kind of ambiguities in Pope, we are likely to misread the poem, "because he expected his readers to prune their minds of any early disorder as carefully as he had pruned his own" (pages 272-273). In particular, Empson suggests that to search for ambiguities of the seventh type in neo-classical poetry is foolish. Finally, Empson does not say whether the guiding principle in muting or not muting ambiguities should be the signals which the poet includes in his work through the function of interinanimation, or whether the decision must be made only after one has achieved a knowledge of literary history – a combination of the two is, obviously, most satisfactory.

It is easy to argue at almost any point with Empson's readings. It is a simple matter to point out flaws and contradictions in such theory as he chooses to set forth. It is true that he often stops at the very point of critical interest and difficulty. Empson's contribution to a theory of metaphor is curious: in terms of philosophically 'earned' principles and distinctions he scores almost zero. Only his statements concerning opposites and muting are set forth with any degree of precision. But the emphasis he gives to ambiguity, particularly to 'meaningful' ambiguity, the vigilance which he arouses in the reader of poetry, and the vast sensitivity which he brings to particular lines establish an attitude toward poetic language which is as valuable, in its own way, as Richards' set of distinctions. Empson points out the limitations of Richard's system, and at the same time makes one aware of the excesses which lack of system may entail.

B. THE TENSION OF ALLEN TATE[6]

For I. A. Richards, teaching is the function of criticism; William Emp-

---

[6] Allen Tate, *The Man of Letters in the Modern World* (New York, 1955). Future references to this book will be included in the text, but since the essays span the years 1928-1955 and have appeared in various places, the year of their

son sees the critic as creating the taste which he also feeds. Allen Tate has a much loftier notion of the role of the man of letters, who may be a poet as well as a critic:

It is the duty of the man of letters to supervise the culture of language, to which the rest of culture is subordinate, and to warn us when our language is ceasing to forward the ends proper to man. The end of social man is communion in time through love, which is beyond time. (page 22, *MLMW*, '52)

Clearly, the man of letters is Allen Tate, and there is no doubt in his mind as to the 'ends proper to man'. The sensibility which produced such a statement is alien to that of the men with whom we have been concerned. It is as though time had suddenly been turned backward, as though once again the universe were metaphysical, psychology once again beneath its four-fold shield, and man labouring through a veil of tears to reach eternal glory. Hulme and Richards and Empson wish to look at literature with the newly awakened wonder of Adam; Tate strives for an awareness as old as the races of man, and for him the business of aesthetics is but a facet of a world view more reminiscent of the tenth than the twentieth century:

Literary criticism, like the Kingdom of God on earth, is perpetually necessary and, in the very nature of its middle position between imagination and philosophy, perpetually impossible. Like a man, literary criticism is nothing in itself; criticism like man, embraces pure experience or exalts pure rationality at the price of abdication from its dual nature. It is of the nature of man and criticism to occupy the intolerable position. Like man's, the intolerable position of criticism has its own glory. It is the only position that it is ever likely to have. (page 174, Is *LCP*, '50-51)

---

first publication will be indicated, and the title of each will be abbreviated after this key:

MLMW —————————	The Man of Letters in the Modern World
L as K ———————————	Literature as Knowledge
T in P ————————————	Tension in Poetry
The SI —————————	The Symbolic Imagination
The AI —————————	The Angelic Imagination
The HF —————————	The Hovering Fly
Is LCP —————————	Is Literary Criticism Possible?
L and NC ————————	Longinus and the "New Criticism"
ED —————————————	Emily Dickinson
N on D ———————————	A Note on Donne
The P of D ———————	The Point of Dying: Donne's Virtuous Men
N on ES —————————	A Not on Elizabethan Satire
JPB —————————————	John Peale Bishop
N as N —————————	Narcissus as Narcissus

And yet beneath the traditional ranguage of religion, there is here essentially the same attitude toward the practical work of criticism that has been noted in Richards and Empson.

But whereas Richards and Empson are more or less in favor of science and 'progress', Tate sees the last three hundred years as a mistake, and the same conditions and attitudes which vitiate life are grave dangers to poetry and criticism: man is no longer possessed of a unified vision. In religion this produces secularism, in poetry symbolism. And yet the multiple vision of modern man is the edge of chaos which makes the best literature. Tate's examples are John Donne and Emily Dickinson, and he sees the very passing of belief which he laments as the source of their creative power:

In Miss Dickinson, as in Donne, we may detect a singularly morbid concern, not for religious truth, but for personal revelation. The modern word is self-exploitation. It is egoism grown irresponsible in religion and decadent in morals. In religion it is blasphemy; in society it means usually that culture is not self-contained and sufficient, that the spiritual community is breaking up. This is . . . the perfect literary situation. (page 221, *ED*, '32)

A paradox is involved; Dickinson and Donne seem modern and relevant because they reflect a kinship to our thoroughly degenerate age: "the 'message' of modern art . . . is that social man is living, without religion, morality, or art (without the high form that concentrates all three in an organic whole), in a mere system of money references through which neither artist nor plutocrat can perform as an entire person" (page 315, *PLS*, '35). Though the attitude is different, this is essentially the view which Richards and Empson take of man's situation, though they do not judge it evil, but rather glory in the opportunities for multiple experience which it provides. Against Dickinson and Donne, Tate sets Dante and Milton, two who produced the 'high moral form' of art which concentrates religion, morality, and art into 'an organic whole'. There is some confusion as to which of the sets Tate prefers. His theology chooses Dante, but his aesthetic instinct prefers Donne.

Tate is a critical Manichean. The power of darkness is great, and it has come to control the creative-perceptive act to the exclusion of the power of light. The effects of darkness may be seen in the 'Angelic imagination', those of light in the 'Symbolic imagination'. Of the first, the literary fathers are Edgar Allan Poe and Samuel Taylor Coleridge (the original father is Lucifer). Through the Angelic imagination man seeks to reach beyond himself, and in breaking the chain of being, he is guilty of *hybris:*

"Imagination is, possibly in man," says Poe . . . "a lesser degree of the creative power of God." This is not far from the "esemplastic power" of the Primary Imagination, a Teutonic angel inhabiting a Cartesian machine named Samuel Taylor Coleridge. (page 124, The AI, '51)

Poe's imagination is Angelic and "his extravagant claims for poetry do not in any particular exceed . . . the claims made by two later generations of English critics represented by Arnold and Richards" (page 124, the AI, '51). The legions are forming on the fiery shore. Descartes calls them, and defiant arms are raised against the 'true way'. Their chief flaw is that because they seek to transcend themselves they have an "uncertain grasp of the relation of language to feeling, and of feeling to nature" (page 117, The AI, '51).

Tate's answer as the guardian of man's true course is clear:

The human intellect cannot reach God as essence; only God as analogy. Analogy to what? Plainly analogy to the natural world; for there is nothing in the intellect that has not previously reached it through the senses . . . . The reach of our imaginative enlargement is perhaps no longer than the ladder of analogy, at the top of which we may see all, if we still wish to *see* anything, that we have brought up with us from the bottom, where lies the sensible world. (page 131, The AI, '51)

This is a curious phrasing of Richards' idea of the engram, but the result is just that. What Tate is objecting to is "the Cartesian split – taste [which should be] feeling respect for the depth of nature, [is instead] resolved into a subjectivism which denies the sensible world; for nature has become geometrical, at a high level of abstraction, in which 'clear and distinct ideas' only are workable" (page 122, The AI, '51). This is to place on Richards' brand of subjectivism a fault from which it does not suffer. Tate is objecting to, in Hulme's terms, the tendency to see experience in terms of extensive manifolds. Richards shares this objection.

Tate lays claim to critical skepticism, but it is a limited sort of skepticism. Like Empson he thinks that the reasons of poetry may be reasoned about, but the limitation of reason must be constantly acknowledged. The method by which man may reason about his condition (and by implication the critic may reason about poetry) is the Symbolic imagination. It, as might be expected, is the opposite of the Angelic imagination. The Symbolic imagination emphasizes feeling, rather than intellect and will: "it is through feeling alone that we witness the glory of our servitude to the natural world of sense. . . . I call that human imagination angelic which tries to distintegrate or to circumvent the image in the illusory pursuit of essence" (page 97, The SI, '51). This, in Hulme's terms, is a plea for the recognition of intensive manifolds.

The method of the Symbolic imagination is apparently the same as that which Richards attributes to metaphor, and which Empson names as the seventh type of ambiguity: "To bring together various meanings at a single moment of action" (page 96, The SI, '51). Perhaps a difference is that Tate insists on the primacy of action: "The symbolic imagination conducts an action through analogy, of the human to the divine, of the natural to the supernatural, of the low to the high, of time to eternity." And even this difference is diminished when Tate makes it clear that action may be other than physical. The net effect of the distinction between Angelic and Symbolic imagination is an insistence that a poet must 'render' his scenes. That he must not expect the reader to supply the details, that he must recreate, not name, the emotion which he wishes to convey. Tate is aware that "the sea boils and pigs have wings because in poetry all things are possible – if you are man enough. They are possible because in poetry the disparate elements are not combined in logic, which can join things only under certain categories and under the law of contradiction; they are combined in poetry rather as experience, and experience has decided to ignore logic . . ." (page 337, N as N, '38). This again suggests Richards; the idea of the superiority of poetic experience is based upon its freedom from the limitations of action and its emancipation from 'fact'.

It seems to me that Tate's quarrel with Richards is based upon Richards' use of the terms of affective psychology which, along with Richards' angelic tone, are anathema to Tate. He gives a very brief summary of his objections to Richards in "The Angelic Imagination":

[Richards] tells us that the pseudo-statements of poetry – poetry on its own – cannot stand against the "certified scientific statement" about the facts which for Arnold had already failed both religion and poetry. Nevertheless poetry will save us because it "orders our minds" – but with what? For Mr. Richards, twenty-five years ago, the Cartesian machine was doing business as usual. Poetry would have to save us by ordering our minds with something that was not true. (page 124, '51)

This objection is no more serious than a problem of diction. Truth and falsehood are opposites. Fact and fiction are opposites. Not all facts are true and not all fictions are false. This is simplistic, but the disagreement between Richards and Tate on this point seems no more vital.

According to Tate there are two modes of poetic creation, the

Angelic (destructive) and the Symbolic (constructive). When he turns his attention from the creation to the perception of a poem, he makes a similar distinction. That distinction, he says, is evident in Coleridge's work:

There is, then, in Coleridge's poetic theory a persistent dilemma. *He cannot make up his mind whether the specifically poetic element is an objective feature of the poem, or is distinguishable only as a subjective effect.* He cannot, in short, choose between metaphysics and psychology. His general emphasis is psychological, with metaphysical ambiguities. (page 55, L as K, '41)

Richards, as we have seen, found in Coleridge a solution to the problem of where 'aesthetic' resides; clearly beauty is in the mind of the reader, but without the stimuli of the artifact, the beauty cannot be perceived. Of the forces which he felt contending in Coleridge, Tate chooses metaphysics. At first this does not seem consistent with his idea of the limitations of man's knowledge, but given Tate's preference for a study of accidents rather than essences, for analogy rather than creation, it follows that he should choose that mode of reading which concentrates on the stimulus rather than the response. Here lies his essential difference with Richards, and to a lesser degree, with Empson.

Richards preferred to investgiate the response. In theory Richards asserts that it is futile to study the artifact in hopes of determining the nature of beauty, but in practice he often makes the attempt. Tate is willing to grant the affective premise, but rather than attempting to follow aesthetic to its source in the mind of the perceiver, he wishes to observe and evaluate the stimulus as bearing within it the seed of a particular kind of response. He makes it clear, however, that he sees the value of affective theory:

It is, in fact, no mere quibble of idealism if we decide to call this subjective field not only the world but the actual world, taking our stand on the assumption that it sufficiently reflects or gathers in or contains all that we can ever know of any other world or worlds that appear to lie beyond it. (page 150, The HF, '43)

The path which Tate chooses between the poem as affective and the poem as artifact is a slippery one. On the one hand the poem itself (the marks on the page) is all that is available for sensible speculation. On the other hand, he realizes that the only way in which the poem is available at all is through the sensibility of the reader working on its own past experiences. He does not wish to choose either, but since an emphasis must be established, he concentrates on the formal elements of the poem. The two figures whom Tate sees as the originators of these positions are Aristotle and Longinus. Aristotle in his concern with pity and terror is the affectivist. Longinus, on the other hand, achieves his considerable originality by "shifting the center of critical interest, without rejecting it as an 'interest', from the genetic and moral judgment to the aesthetic, from the subject matter and the psychology of the author to the language of the work" (page 187, L and NC, '48).

Richards, says Tate, belongs with Aristotle:

Mr. Richard's books may be seen together as a parable, as a mythical and dramatic projection, of the failure of the modern mind to understand poetry on the assumptions underlying the demireligion of positivism. We do not need to reject the positive and rational mode of inquire into poetry . . . . [But] we must return to, we must never leave, the poem itself. Its "interest" value is a cognitive one; it is sufficient that here, in the poem, we get knowledge of a whole object. If rational inquiry is the only mode of criticism, we must yet remember that the way we apply that mode must always powerfully affect our experience of the poem . . . . However we may see the completeness of poetry, it is a problem less to be solved than in its full import, to be preserved. (page 63, L as K, '41)

If it is true that Richards' method fails, then the question to be answered is, "Can there be a criticism of convincing objectivity which approaches the literary work through the analysis of style and which arrives at its larger aspects through that aperture?" (page 179, L and NC, '48). "Yes", says Tate, with reservations. The basic assumption is that "good poetry can bear the closest literal examination of every phrase, and is its own safegard against our irony" (page 67, T in P, '38). 'Close reading' is the only way in which anything about a poem can be known, for "the poem is its own knower, neither poet nor reader [know] anything that the poem says apart from the words of the poem" (page 333, N as N, '38).

Longinus, says Tate, attempts this method in his comments on Sappho: "*He is trying to see what is happening in the poem.* If he is hampered by his affective terms, so was Mr. T. S. Eliot when, in an early essay, he was getting at a similar play of opposites (what Mr. Cleanth Brooks has since called 'paradox') by proposing his theory of the 'positive' and 'negative' emotion . . ." (page 186, L and NC, '48). Tate says that Eliot was writing "advanced romantic criticism: it was struggling through the subjective effect towards the objective structure of the work". The important thing is to shift the attention from what the poem 'feels like' to what it 'says'. Richards has made it plain that these two cannot be separated. What the poem 'feels like' is part of what it 'says'. However, to give the 'feel' without the 'says' is much worse, and more useless as criticism, than to give the 'says' without the 'feel'. The unity of the two is shown very clearly in the readings which make up the bulk of *Seven Types of Ambiguity*.

Tate's basic skepticism keeps him from claiming that close reading will yield the ultimate poetic meaning. "The high order of the poetic insight is that the final insight must elude us . . . it sees not only with but through the natural world, to what may lie beyond it" (page 112, The SI, '51). This sounds like the paradox of Blake's multiple vision, and it is, of course, Angelic, but then so is Man. That point at which Tate starts is diametrically opposed to Richards' assumptions, but the result is not so different. Like Hulme, like Richards, and like Empson, Allen Tate sees the function of poetry as one of annealing the disparities of existence. He recognizes the multiplicity of man, of man's environment, and of the perception of that environment. But whereas Hulme and Richards see the mind as a unifying organ, Tate conceives of our natural mode of perception as a tendency to divide, to see things as opposites:

We are so constituted as to see our experience in two ways. We are not so constituted as to see it in two ways indefinitely without peril. Until we can see it in one way we shall not see it as a whole, and until we see it as a whole we shall not see it as poets. Every road is long, and all roads lead to the problem of form. (page 276, JPB, '35)

What unity of vision man can have of a poem must be through form, but it is not form divorced from content. The division of poetry into container and the thing contained is simply another face of seeing 'experience in two ways', and if the perception of the poem is to have unity, the distinction must be obliterated. But, of course, since there is (in Tate's imperfect world) no such thing as a perfect poem, the fusion of form and content is imperfect. It would appear that despite man's best efforts, the 'peril' of divisive vision is omnipresent:

The fusion of art and nature, of technique and subject, can never exceed the approximate; the margin of imperfection, of the unformed, is always there – nature intractable to art, art unequal to nature . . . . There is a reciprocal relation between technique and subject; and they reveal each other. (page 183, L and NC, '48)

Thus, it is the imperfect fusion of form and content that is responsible for the vitality of art. Were it possible to achieve 'perfection' in art, the result would be of little interest to man who is fixed in his dual nature.

It is curious to note how very close the result is to the conclusions of I. A. Richards; though each man violently rejects the terminology of the other, in Tate's words, "all roads lead to the problem of form". Richards' theory of the interinanimation of words SOUNDS very different from Tate's speculations upon the source of meaning, but the two are essentially the same:

The powers of language were not in the long run determined by theory, but instinctively by poets whose dominating passion was form: the language was determined by the demands of the subject. The more comprehensive the subject, the broader the symbolism, and the more profoundly relevent the scheme of references to the whole human experience, the richer the language became .... For form is meaning and nothing but meaning; scheme of reference, supporting symbolism that ceases to support as soon as it is re- cognized as merely that. (page 269, JPB, '35)

Though essentially this is a definition of meaning as the 'total of the missing parts of its context', the attitude is different than Richards'; Tate is saying "we murder to dissect", which contrasts sharply with his statement that poetry "can bear the closest literal examination of every phrase".

Allen Tate is caught between the unitive vision which he desires and the divisive vision which all men possess. Things do not fuse, and yet it is 'wrong' to think of them separately. It is curious that after he has so strongly insisted on the necessity of unity, on the vice which results from taking things apart, from looking at intensive manifolds as though they were extensive, Tate should follow exactly that method in his most important formulation of the workings of language. For angelic man, there is no other way. His term for the basic poetic quality is 'tension', a term which denies unity and rather asserts a balance of conflicting forces:

... the term *tension*. I am using the term not as a general metaphor, but as a special one, derived from lopping the prefixes off the logical terms *ex*- tension and *in*tension. What I am saying, of course, is that the meaning of poetry is its "tension," the full organized body of all the extension and in- tension that we can find in it. The remotest figurative significance that we can derive does not invalidate the extensions of the literal statement. Or we may begin with the literal statement and by stages develop the complications of metaphor: at every stage we may pause to state the meaning so far apprehended, and at every stage the meaning will be coherent. (page 70, T in P, '38)

Extension is denotation; intension is connotation. The only value of substituting the less for the more familiar terms is that they provide a middle term, 'tension', which suggests that the two must be considered together, though not exactly as one. Despite the insistence that 'tension' resides in the poem itself and that we 'derive' our perception of it from the marks on the page, Tate realizes that poetic perception is not quite that simple: "The meanings that we select at different points along the infinite line between extreme intension and extreme extension will vary with our personal 'drive', or 'interest', or 'approach' (page 70, T in P, '38). Here is Richards' engram. The major difference is in terminology.

The operation of 'tension' is quite simple, at least in theory. Tate constructs a continuum with extension (denotation) at one end and intension (connotation) at the other:

The metaphysical poet as a rationalist begins at or near the extensive or denoting end of the line; the romantic or Symbolist poet at the other, intensive end; and each by a straining feat of the imagination tries to push his meanings as far as he can towards the opposite end, so as to occupy the entire scale. (page 76, T in P)

This is reminiscent of Hulme's metaphor of the architect's curves, and like Hulme, Tate tells us nothing about that 'straining feat of the imagination', but rather presents a series of touchstones. "These touchstones, I believe, are not poetry of the extremes, but poetry of the center: poetry of tension, in which the 'strategy' is diffused into the unitary effect" (page 74, T in P, '38). Tension is not the peculiar quality of any single kind of poetry. His touchstones cover almost every sort of lyric, with the exception of neo-classical, and it would be possible to extend his list to include Pope without violating the quality he calls tension.[7] Tate's tension is very like the last of Empson's ambiguities, and he acknowledges the similarity:

In metaphysical poetry the logical order is explicit; it must be coherent; the imagery by which it is sensuously embodied must have at least the appearance of logical determinism: perhaps the appearance only, because the varieties of ambiguity and contradiction possible beneath the logical surface are endless, as Mr. Empson's elucidation of Marvell's "The Garden" has shown. Here it is enough to say that the development of imagery by extension, its logical determinants being an Ariadne's thread that the poet will not permit us to lose, is the leading feature of the poetry called metaphysical. (page 68, T in P, '38)

If there is a difference between Tate and Empson on this point, it is that Empson is less a dualist. Empson does not divide the poem into

[7] Cleanth Brooks' essay, "The Case of Miss Arabella Fermor", *The Well Wrought Urn* (New York, 1947), pp. 80 ff, does just this.

'structure' and 'texture' or 'ex-in-tension' and then seek a unity in 'sensuous embodiment'. Empson's attitude achieves more nearly the unitive vision which Tate seeks than does Tate's theory. And yet they both see that reading and criticism are arts, not sciences. In Empson's words, "so far as a critic has made himself dispassionate about [poetry], so far as he has repressed sympathy in favour of curiosity, he has made himself incapable of examining it" (*Seven Types*, page 280).

Allen Tate calls the study of metaphor the '*pons asinorum*' of criticism. "Everybody is unsatisfactory, even Mr. I. A. Richards, whose *Philosophy of Rhetoric* offers a good deal but promises too much. This is a field of inquiry of a difficulty equal to that of the burden of the mystery" (page 190, L and NC, '48). Tate begins his discussion with Chapter XXII of Aristotle's *Poetics*: "But the greatest thing by far is to be a master of metaphor. It is the one thing that cannot be learnt from others; and it is also a sign of genius, since a good metaphor implies an intuitive perception of the similarity in dissimilars." But although for Tate this is "very nearly the beginning and end of our own inquiries into metaphor", he is not content to allow Aristotle to mean what he says:

I am rash enough to question whether Aristotle as a Greek, could know, as we have known since Shakespeare and Donne, how similar dissimilars can be made to seem, of (to take an extreme view not unknown today) how similar they can be made to be . . . . Metaphor by analogy takes the formula of arithmetical proportion, a quantitative and rational procedure. We are thus in the Greek Cosmos, and ordering of solid objects under a physics of motion in which the formal object offers but a narrow margin of analogy to any other . . . . Our multiverse has increasingly since the seventeenth century, consisted of unstable objects dissolving into energy; and there has been no limit to the extension of analogy. (pages 191-192, L and NC, '48)

Tate suggests that Aristotle's definition is of what we refer to as simile (in effect, not form), rather than of metaphor. Aristotle sees metaphor as an assertion of similarities; Tate suggests that it asserts identification. In his discussion of Donne's "A Valediction: Forbidding Mourning", he states the essential unity of tenor and vehicle:

Donne is not saying that death is *like* love, or that love is *like* death; there is the identity, death-love, a third something, a reality that can be found only through analogy since it has no name . . . . This reality, whether of "dying" lovers or of "dying" men, is the ultimate experience. The reciprocal conversion of the one into the other is the moral motion of the poem, its peripety, the "action" which eventually issues in the great toplevel significance that Donne understood as the anagoge. (page 248, The P of D, '52)

This 'third' something is effective because of the resistances of the mind to an identity which is outside reason, and yet not unreasonable. 'Death love', though not a fact, is a truth. Although metaphor is the most striking instance of tension in poetry, Tate sees the "controlled distortions of literal representation" (page 69), as inherent in all the devices of poetry:

It is this resistance of the language to full expression, the strain between images and rhythm, opposites "yoked by violence together" in varying degrees of violence, that gives to English lyrical verse its true genius . . . . It is that quality of English style which is superior to age and school. (page 254, N on ES, '32)

Although he begins from a point of view which is antithetical to the assumptions of Hulme, of Richards, and of Empson, Tate manages to arrive at a position which is strikingly similar. It is reassuring to see that the direction of thought which we have been following in the New Critics is not ultimately at odds with traditional beliefs. Stripped of its theological trappings, the criticism of Allen Tate provides a useful refinement in a Ricardian theory of metaphor.

C. THE IRRELEVANT HETEROGENEITY OF JOHN C. RANSOM

The New Criticism[8] is the first of a series of books which attempts to summarize, synthesize, and correct the theories of those who have come to be known as 'New Critics'. At the same time the book presents a philosophical position and a number of terms which carry forward the work which Richards began. No more than Tate or Empson does Ransom deny the importance of his great progenitor, but he sees certain excesses of theory and emphasis which need correction. In many ways the book parallels Richards' *Philosophy of Rhetoric*: there is the same definition and application of terms, the same concentration on theory with an effort to keep, at every point, in touch with existing poetic structures. And yet the two books are quite different in assumption. Richards admits the necessity of speaking of neural, physiological events as if they occurred outside the mind; only occasionally does he forget that his comments on metaphor are convenient external illustrations for psychic phenomena. Ransom proceeds in the opposite fashion. Most of the time he considers the poem to be an artifact, complete in

[8] John Crowe Ransom, *The New Criticism*. Future page references are included in the text.

itself. Only occasionally does he acknowledge that a poem is a symbol for a reference which is at the same time the referent, and that as such, a substantial part of the poem as perceived must, because of the varied experiences of readers, be subjective.

He begins his discussion of the New Criticism by suggesting corrections for the work which has gone before:

Briefly, the new criticism is damaged by at least two specific errors of theory, which are widespread. One is the idea of using the psychological affective vocabulary in the hope of making literary judgments in terms of feeling, emotions, and attitudes of poems instead of in terms of their object. The other is plain moralism, which in the new criticism would indicate that it has not emancipated itself from the old criticism. I should like to see critics unburdened of these drags. (page xi)

The second error, moralism, he discusses at length in his chapter on Yvor Winters, and though it might be taken as a caution against the moralism of Tate as well, his warnings against moralism are outside the scope of the present study.

The first error refers to the influence of Richards' affective vocabulary. It is significant that Ransom does not here deny the validity of Richards' theory, but only objects to the imprecision of vocabulary. He does, however, wish to deal with the poem as artifact, and so must attempt to refute Richards' definition of a poem as a balance of impulses:

I should think there is generally, and ideally, no emotion at all until an object has furnished the occasion for one, and that the critic is faking his discovery of the emotion he cannot make out its object; and that if he should try to describe to us the emotion he would find himself describing it as whatever kind of emotion would be appropriate towards a certain object, and therefore presently, before he realized it, beginning to describe the very object which he had meant to avoid. (pages 20-21)

This is most certainly true, but it does not contradict in any significant way Richards' theories of the perception of poetry. The difference is in emphasis; like Tate, Ransom wishes to concentrate on the stimulus rather than upon the response, though ultimately he realizes that comments concerning the nature of the object which serves as stimulus are valuable only insofar as they provide insight into the quality of response. When he seems to be denying the reality of affective experience, he is only asking that the critic concentrate on the object which produces the response, for an understanding of the objective correlative of affective states.

Ransom is not unaware of Richards' solution to this problem, but for reasons of poetic strategy he rejects it, or at least tries to do so. He notes the third and fourth definitions which Richards suggests for beauty: the third assumes that certain tertiary qualities in an object (proportion or unity, for example) make it beautiful; the fourth assumes that there is an undefinable kernel within an object which provides the occasion for a perception which may be called beautiful, given certain conditions within the perceiver.[9] Richards chooses the fourth as the most accurate description of the source of beauty. Ransom disagrees:

To this argument it may be replied that the subjective definition offered for beauty . . . at the fourth degree of sophistication is scarcely more intelligible than the one offered at the third degree. But, more urgently still, it may be replied that our predicament in the fourth degree is too painful. I should wish to remain in the third degree of sophistication a long time rather than to be sophisticated into intellectual paralysis. (page 54)

Despite his rejection here of the fourth degree, Ransom notes two dangers involved in its sophistication and then proceeds with it as the basis of his criticism. The first of his warnings is directed at the poet: the fourth degree of sophistication may tempt him to try a direct expression of emotion, rather than to present a situation which will allow the reader to reconstruct an approximation of that emotion. In such a case the short-cut results in sentimentality:

A sentimental poet . . . must be the poet who neglects the complete communication of his occasion, and for a short-cut pronounces the affective words that the reader should pronounce for himself, and then only on the understanding that they were appropriate to a communication that has been received. (page 51)

This accords very well with Richards' definition of the sentimental poem, and is parallel to Tate's idea of the result of Angelic imagination. It is the need for a Jamesian 'rendering'. The poet must earn his emotion.

The second danger is for the critic/reader: the fourth degree requires him to distinguish, constantly, between 'objective' and 'subjective', to be at all times aware of the subjective nature of his evidence. Ransom says that this awareness constitutes 'a very embarrassing policy' that is "especially mortal to the objective side of analysis" (page 26). Of

[9]   The four possible places of beauty are presented by Richards in *Practical Criticism: A Study of Literary Judgment* (New York, 1929), p. 359. The first degree assumes that all beauty resides in the artifact. The second that all beauty is in the mind of the beholder.

course it is, but to ignore the problem is not to solve it, nor will it go away if its existence is not acknowledged. It is clear that Ransom realizes this, but it is equally clear that he wishes the problem away:

The affections are involved by a poem, but the important thing for theory to see is that they attach spontaneously to the items of context. And since they attach spontaneously, they scarcely need to enter into critical discussion. We need only to say that the poem develops its local particularities while it progresses towards its functional completion. (page 58)

So long as the critic realizes, as does Ransom, that affective theory accounts for the basic nature of the perception of poetry, and that the exciting of emotion in the reader is poetry's primary goal, there is little to be lost and much to be gained in concentrating on 'the poem itself'. The fallacy involved in the subjective nature of reading may be granted, silently, as analysis proceeds AS THOUGH the poem were an object.

Once this qualification is made, Ransom's criticism is as basic as one could wish. He attempts to define poetry, to isolate its components, to explain their interactions, and finally to suggest the reasons for poetry's existence:

In what world of discourse does it [the poem] have its existence? As a thing of sounds it exists in the words; as a thing of meanings it exists in a world beyond the words. The heterogeneity is rather extreme. We recall the old puzzle, the debate on whether the poem resides in the physical words said or in the interpretation that is given them. But it exists in both at once; and for fear we forget about the words, they are metered, so that they may be forced upon our attention. (pages 328-329)

Nothing here contradicts Richards' definition of the 'fourth degree of sophistication', but Ransom has shifted the emphasis from the response rather to the stimulus. His definition of a beautiful poem takes into account those very elements which he seemed to condemn in Richards:

A beautiful poem is an objective discourse
which we approve, containing objective detail
which we like.

This version mixes objective and subjective terms, but goes much further than simply to say that poetry is a form of discourse which enlists our favorable emotions. It tells where the favorable emotions come: in the pleasure of handling the specific detail while we are attending effectively to the whole .... The definition calls for a poetic "texture" without trying to have one outside logical discourse. (pages 54-55)

Despite this assertion of unity, the effect of Ransom's criticism is to provide for separate modes of discourse existing within the same poem.

In his distinction between objective discourse and objective detail, Ransom creates a dichotomy parallel to Richards' distinction between 'tenor' and 'vehicle', and to Tate's distinction between 'extension' and 'intension'. The three sets of distinctions are complementary: the combination of tenor and vehicle results in metaphor, a relatively narrow category concerned primarily with diction. The combination of extension and intension results in tension (Empson's ambiguity), a broader category concerned with both syntax and diction. Structure and texture is a yet broader distinction, including syntax, diction, meter, and meaning; the combination of structure and texture produces a poem. All three critics are careful to assert that they make their distinctions in theory only, and that in practice neither half of their dichotomies can exist without the other half. Thus they preserve the unity of the poem and of poetic experience. But all three systems are dualistic.

The idea of warring structure and texture is not new. In *Biographia Literaria*, Coleridge seems to be saying much the same thing as Ransom says in *The New Criticism*: "In Shakespeare's *poems*, the creative power and the intellectual energy wrestle as in a war embrace. Each in its excess of strength seems to threaten the extinction of the other" (Chapter XV). But Coleridge is quite sure that the battle is bad, and he does not see fit to pursue the implications. Ransom sees the 'war embrace' as the dominant creative act. Its strategy is most clearly stated in Ransom's theory of the struggle between meaning and sound. I shall quote at length because the basic relationship is the same when Ransom applies the structure-texture tool to matters of imagery:

A poet must do two things at once; one is to make a logical structure, the other is to make meter. The logical structure is ordinarily the meaning that he starts with, having its appropriate words. But there is the meter, a purely phonetic pattern, which requires its appropriate words too, and cannot accept every word that comes. The meaning-words have to be manipulated, and altered, in order to suit the meter. Eventually the poem is done. In it now the relation of the meter to the meaning is that of a texture to a structure; this texture is adventitious, and irrelevant to the structure, but highly visible, and to the innocent reader like a curious increment of riches that has not been bargained for. But the finished poem will have even more important texture than the phonetic. It will have texture of meaning too, and it is the requirement of attending to the meters in the act of composing the meaning that secures this too. Tinkering with the words loosens up the logic, introducing periphrases, ellipses, inaccuracies, and, what is more valuable, importations. In trying to find for the logical detail a substitute that will suit the meter, the poet will discover presently that the best way is to explore this detail to see what it contains, and to come up with facts which belong to the detail but not to the logical structure; and nothing in poetry is so remarkable as this. It is the thing that particularly qualifies a discourse as being poetic; it is its differentia. The fact of this non-structural increment of meaning is, I think, what critics need most to attest. (pages 219-220)

Ransom's dualism is less resolved than that of Richards and Tate. And he sees the lack of resolution as one of poetry's greatest strengths. For instance, he does not believe that the meter really 'echoes the sense' in any meaningful way. Rather, it has a separate existence from the meaning and tends to interfere with the prose sense which the poet attempts. "But since the logic survives, then we have a phonetic discourse operating at once with the same words. That is a phenomenon fairly exciting to our speculative interest . . ." (page 30). And it is essential to preserve the duality of discourse, for if the meter is perfectly directed by the sense, the result is prose. "Meter is like metaphor: the moment the metaphor is perfectly subdued to its logical function in the meaning it ceases to be metaphor" (page 259).[10] As might be expected, Ransom's dualism leads him to theorize upon the relative importance of structure and texture – a system which denies their unification makes it necessary to assign primacy to one or the other. This judging leads to a number of problems which can be solved only by understanding that for Ransom the terms are functional, not ontological; they refer to the role which a particular item is playing when viewed from a particular vantage.[11] Thus there is a structure-texture relationship at any particular point at which attention is fixed. The basic, or largest, division is one which might be called form and content. But within the form there is texture, created by the variations from the basic pattern of the meter which are forced by the content. And within the content (which is texture when viewed in its relationship with form) there is a war embrace between what the poet wishes to say and the recalcitrancy of the words which he must use to say it. The same procedure obtains right down the line: to the single word of 'meaning', and to the single poetic foot of 'form'. If Richards' terms, vehicle and tenor, are also viewed as functional, the confusion in difficult cases as to which is tenor, which vehicle, can be understood. The problem with the functional solution which Ransom proposes is that it is necessary to decide which of the contesting elements formed the basis for the struggle and which was

[10]   This extreme case is what I have called 'positive metaphor'. See Chapter Four, A, below.
[11]   It is not unusual for critics to miss this distinction. A fairly recent example is Richard Foster, *The New Romantics*, p. 139.

the intrusive element. Such a decision moves toward the intentional fallacy.

Our natural instinct, says Ransom, is to prefer the meaning to the sound, and so the poet must spend his energies battling the recalcitrant form, but of course the content can be expressed in no other way. "The texture of a poem is the heterogeneous character of its detail, which either fills in the logical outline very densely or else overflows it a little" (page 163), and of course if there is nothing to fill nor to over-flow, no texture can exist. Structure and texture interact, but it is always the structure which generates the texture – even though the texture often turns out to be the more interesting. From this Ransom concludes that the basic requirement of a poem is a paraphrasable content:

Often, and perhaps usually, we are unable to take much pride in the mere paraphrase or argument of the poem by itself; yet the paraphrase is a fair version of the logical structure. The "arguments" of the poems are apt to seem rather commonplace. They have as a rule less distinction, not more distinction, than the prose arguments that are able to stand by themselves; and they are not meant to stand by themselves. The arguments are for the sake of the poem; without arguments there can be no poems. (page 269)

This is Richards' 'pseudo-statements' much modified; Ransom's version is the more satisfactory. Ransom sees an inverse proportion operating between structure and texture: "the more difficult the final structure, the less rich should be the distraction of the texture; and the richer the texture as we proceed towards the structure, the more generalized and simple may be the structure in the end" (page 274). This may be visual-ized as a straight line (structure) which is constantly being forced to make zig-zags (texture) perpendicular to its basic direction. A graph of a poem, then, would look very like the picture of speech given by an oscillograph; the more vertical lines, the richer the texture, but the more irrelevancies to the structure. The poem "is a loose logical struc-ture with an irrelevant local texture" (page 280). Ransom realizes that 'irrelevant' is not quite the right word, for despite the apparent lack of relation, "any detail has all its facets of particularity, and is so hetero-geneous that it will attach somewhere to the logical interest which the poet is developing" (page 113). Empson provides adequate documenta-tion for this. There is always the question of whether the poet failed to provide or the reader failed to perceive the proper connections.

Generally, Ransom makes the stubborness of texture something against which the poet must fight. A paradox is involved. Since Ran-som's view of life is quite like that suggested for Empson – that is, a

series of balances and imbalances between multiple opposing forces –
it would appear that the more skillful a poet becomes in subduing texture to structure, the less relevant would be his presentation of experience. Ransom, in a diagram worthy of Richards, anticipates this
objection. The skilled poet:

likes the variations regardless of the meanings, finding them essential in the
capacity of sound texture to go with the sound structure. It is no very late
stage of a poet's advancement that his taste rejects a sustained phonetic regu-
larity as something restricted and barren, perhaps ontologically defective. Ac-
cordingly he is capable of writing smooth meters and then roughening them
on purpose. And it must be added, while we are about it, that he is capable
of writing a clean logical argument, and then roughening that too, by introducing logical violence into it, and perhaps willful obscurity. We have
therefore this unusual degree of complexity in the total structure: the indeterminate sound or the indeterminate meaning . . . may have been really
come to independently by a poet who senses the aesthetic value of indeter-
minateness and is veteran enough to be straight after it. (pages 324-325)

Ransom considers this structure-texture relationship to be important
not only for the poet in the act of creation, but for criticism as well:

To define the structure-texture procedure of poets is to define poetic strategy, the last and rarest gift that is given to poets . . . . I do not suppose that
analytic studies of other men's invention would make all the difference for
those who are not themselves inventive. But as for the critic, these studies
would put him for the first time in possession of an inside understanding
of his art-words. I do not think that other studies can do that. (page 275)

At the very least such an examination would cause the critic to focus
his attention very closely upon the poem. Ransom's system, if it does
nothing else, encourages the sort of 'close-reading' which is associated
with the New Criticism. Ransom's claim of the importance of indeter-
minateness is made upon the basis of a conception of poetry and life
which links him with Hulme, Richards, and Empson, and which is
quite unlike the asserted belief of Tate:

The objects that go into a poem are heterogeneous, or many-sided, many-
valued. All objects are really so, and may be considered to remain so even
when we assemble objects together. In a structural assemblage the principle
of assembly is of course the one or more aspects in respect to which the
objects are uniform; we waive the heterogeneity and keep the uniformity.
But a poem attends to the uniformity without waiving the heterogeneity.
(page 92)

As he asserts the separateness of sound and sense, he reveals the nature
of his conception of life:

The law is an ontological one: the two properties shall not be identical, or like, or homogeneous, they shall be other, unlike, and heterogeneous. It is the law of the actual world everywhere; all sorts of actual things are composed on this principle. It is only the naive prejudice of our first way of thought, our Eleatic stage of thought, that makes us conceive that the properties must unite by virtue of their sameness. (page 327)

Here is the ultimate justification for irrelevant texture: the world is full of irrelevancies and to leave them out of the world of the poem is to give a false picture of both worlds.

The relationships between Ransom's 'heterogeneity' and Empson's 'ambiguity' are interesting. Although Ransom realizes that Empson means many different things by 'ambiguity', he prefers to think of ambiguity as opposed to "diffuseness – the scattering of attention over the field of local particularity" (page 103). Ransom suggests (though it might be difficult to prove from Empson's varied comments on ambiguity) that ambiguity in some degree insists upon a relationship among all possible meanings; even if that relationship is only one of Freudian opposites. Diffuseness (by which Ransom means heterogeneity) insists "that opposites can never be said to be resolved or reconciled merely because they have been got into the same poem, or got into the same complex of affective experience to create a kind of 'tension' (page 95).

The idea of heterogeneity represents the greatest departure which Ransom makes from the ideas of Richards, Empson, and Tate. Tate's metaphor of the ladder of analogy is an assertion of the basic unity of the universe; it suggests that heterogeneity is the result of human imperfection and that once man has climbed the ladder, he can view the essential unity which God created.[12] Ransom suggests that it is man's imperfection which makes him insist on seeing unity where none exists. It was suggested above that a haiku rests upon acceptance rather than upon unification. According to Ransom the function of the poet is to present heterogeneous materials for acceptance, as well as ambiguous materials for unification. Though the latter, unified vision, is possible, it is by no means universal:

We should be so much in favor of tragedy and irony as not to think it good policy to require them in all our poems, for fear we might bring them into bad fame .... Tragedy suggests Irony, and Irony leads easily to Ambiguity. (page 101)

---

[12] This idea is set forth at length in Tate's pair of essays, "The Symbolic Imagination" and "The Angelic Imagination". See Chapter Two, B, above.

Empson's theory is so heterogeneous as to avoid the Eleatic flaw, but Ransom finds him, in practice, guilty of searching for and supplying relationships where none exist (page 129).

John Crowe Ransom, like the other critics who have been discussed, finds metaphor to be "the expert and most characteristic method employed by the poet for communicating feelings . . ." (page 50). And it is in the combinations and permutations which he achieves among tenor, vehicle, structure, and texture that he makes his most significant contribution to a theory of metaphor. He quickly disposes of the Aristotle-Johnson conception of metaphor as essentially a recognition of the likeness of unlike things:

In brief, then, a certain direction is imparted to the tenor by the particular vehicle, and this has a genuine bearing on the logical structure; but with it comes an increment of local meaning which is pure texture. The shooting star is not really a part of [Shakespeare's] fleeing Adonis. Beyond the precise point, or points as Richards certainly has the right to find, of the analogy, there is the substantive body of the vehicle. Between this and the body of the tenor it is very hard, in spite of Coleridge and Richards, to find much mutual modification or "interinanimation." (page 83)

This 'irrelevance' is most obvious in those metaphors which give the vehicle in advance of the tenor – in suspended metaphors. Old English riddles work on this principle; for example, "The Bow" gives a number of vehicles before the tenor is named. Since the reader is not allowed to know the points of similarity which he is supposed to see (he cannot see the ground for a metaphorical shift until he has some hint of the tenor), he is forced to hold as many as possible of the connotations and denotations of the vehicle in mind "in order to have the right values ready when they can be used". But once he is given the tenor, the surplus values of the vehicle do not simply evaporate. "The texture will not disappear, but will remain memorable within the mind; perhaps the texture will even define the structure rather than the other way round." Ransom illustrates this suspended metaphor as a sort of mathematical problem: "My tenor is x; it occurs somewhere in each of the following vehicles; find x" (page 124). This is what Brooks, says Ransom, calls 'functional' or 'structural' metaphor.

Ransom does not maintain with much rigor the distinction between ambiguity and heterogeneity which I have isolated in his criticism.[13] He realizes that despite the irrelevance of many of the associations of a

---

[13]   This distinction is similar to Wheelwright's in *Metaphor and Reality*. Wheelwright calls heterogeneity 'diaphoric' and ambiguity 'epiphoric', though he admits that the distinction cannot be maintained with rigor.

particular vehicle to its strictly phrased tenor, there is an essential unity of perception in the reading of poetry: "We do find it possible to construct long lists of possible resemblances between a tenor and its vehicle, and feel ourselves empowered to elect among them. . . . I should call this perhaps the *total theoretical ambiguity of metaphoric usage.*" But such total ambiguity is not, says Ransom, in the best interest of poetry; it results from the Eleatic flaw. It is possible to CONSTRUCT resemblances, "but poetry has rather more logical integrity than that of being a game at inventing comparisons" (pages 130-31). Such shuffling is distressing. Ransom's refusal to use the terms of affective thought prevents him from making a distinction which, though it does not solve the problem, at least sets it forth in comprehensible terms. Empson's insistence that the reader must construct a poem, from, of course, the artifact, but that it must be the RIGHT poem, is more honest than Ransom's equivocation. The problem may well be that he uses 'poem' to mean two things: the artifact, and the response to the artifact. In a sense he is right to mean both by the word 'poem', for poetry cannot exist without both. In general, however, it seems wise to use 'artifact' when speaking of the words on the page and to use 'response' when speaking of the reaction of the reader. This reserves 'poem' for the combination of the two. In affective terms, Ransom's idea would approach this: almost any poetic vehicle 'imports' elements which have no logical connection to the rational tenor, but since all sorts of arational activities occur which are inseparable from cognition, the mind as a 'connecting organ' insists upon adjusting these irrelevancies into some relation to the context. The distinction is between ambiguity (an eventual unification or elimination of disparate meanings) and heterogeneity (simultaneity of perception which acknowledges disparity). Both have unity, but whereas the first has cognitive unity, the second has only the unity of simultaneous perception. All juxtapositions have, by definition, the second kind of unity, but not all need be cognitively related. Cognition, Richards asserts and Ransom admits, is but one of the processes involved in perceiving a metaphor.

Ransom and Richards disagree in ways in which an 'objectivist' and a 'subjectivist' (neither is so foolish as to be strictly one or the other) must disagree when they attempt to understand terms. Ransom, in summarizing his objections to Richards' ideas on metaphor, denies the primacy of the unconscious and the reduction of the will which he finds in Richards and Coleridge (page 77), but his conclusions are quite in accord with Richards' thought:

But poetry [as opposed to science which must be careful to exclude irrelevant analogy] characteristically goes out of and beyond its ostensible argument, and its technique often is analogy. This does not have to be express analogy, such as to put the mind on guard, but sometimes is sly analogy, taking advantage of the hazard of language, and slipping in without advertisement the older and fuller meaning of a word. Behind poetry is the whole loosely articulated body of the language, making available to discourse at nearly any instant the word whose origin was out of a far more concrete occasion than the present one. The act of using the common word induces metaphor in the suggestible poet. (page 79)

Note that Ransom speaks of the POET's creativity. Richards and Empson concern themselves primarily with the READER's creativity. Ransom assumes that a poem means what its creator intended it to mean. If an author writes in a heterogeneous manner, he should be read the same way, and since "heterogeneity is the specific, the characteristic mode of poetry" (page 130), it is inevitable that a critic who operates like Richards or Empson must at times be guilty of overreading: "In over-developing the local occasions of" the logical problem, Empson "is behind his readers in his sense of responsibility for the logical structure in poetry as a whole".

It seems to me extremely important to recognize and approve such logical structure as a poem may have; its texture of meanings should find a structure to attach itself to. The poets are not quite irresponsible, and the readers should not be more irresponsible than the poets. (page 129)

Ransom is here asking for a theory of muting. He suggests that there are two distinct types of metaphor: those which announce the tenor before or at the same time as the vehicle is presented; and those which give elements of the vehicle before the tenor is made clear – in an extreme case the tenor may never be set forth explicitly. The extreme of the second kind – submerged metaphor – requires the reader to discover all possible connotations and denotations. He must then discover, as in a puzzle, that tenor which suits the varied vehicles. But the first kind, in which the tenor is presented at once, requires that the reader focus on those qualities which suit the tenor. Ransom objects to a critic who insists on reading a 'muted-metaphor' as though it were a 'suspended-metaphor'. The only guard which Empson provides against such over-readings is the common sense of the reader. Ransom, by insisting on the poem-as-object, upon artifact, allows the poet to remain in control. We are left with the basic clash between affective and objective aesthetics. The clash is largely theoretical; in practice the poet and the reader use both with amazing agility. It is the 'affectivist' Richards who suggests, with his 'fourth degree of sophistication', a way to make use of the best of both.[14]

Ransom presents two systems which are useful in analyzing metaphor: structure-texture and ambiguity-heterogeneity. His concern for the poet's intention is a useful corrective to Empson's readings. Despite his protests, Ransom's work can be viewed as a logical development of ideas implicit in Richards' thought:

I am not prepared to lay down principles for effectiveness in metaphor, I should feel disposed at the moment to argue for a logical propriety, a specific "point of analogy," as the occasion for any given metaphor; and then for brilliance and importance in the body of the vehicle in its own right. But it seems to be scarcely open to question that the vehicle must realize itself independently and go beyond its occasion. (And I think nowhere does Richards say the contrary.) In doing this the vehicle becomes irrelevant to the structure of the argument, and asserts the poetic undertaking to incorporate local texture. (page 85)

There is no very basic disagreement between Richards and Ransom as to the nature of metaphor. But there is a difference in emphasis. Whereas Richards concentrates on the poem as reaction and the creative activity of the reader, Ransom is concerned with the poem as artifact and the creative activity of the poet. The two are complementary.

D. CLEANTH BROOKS AND THE STRUCTURE OF PARADOX

The critical stance of Cleanth Brooks is much like that of William Empson, though his readings cover a narrower range of poetic strategy and his theories are set forth more clearly. Like Empson (and unlike Tate and Ransom) his work is directed primarily to the reader of poetry, rather than to the writer. Although he is not so willing to give the reader free reign as is Empson, neither is he so concerned about the method of poetic creation as is Ransom. His major statements about metaphor have to do with the function of imagery, rather than with its essence, though he would say that its essence IS its function.

Brooks' most basic attitudes toward the primary problems of aes-

---

[14] Ransom, *Kenyon Review*, XVI (1954), phrases his position somewhat differently. The basic idea is the same, but the new phrasing eliminates something of the dualism suggested by 'structure' and 'texture'. Ransom says that the poem is a world of its own which presents in the relationships which exist among its components an ontological knowledge of the world in which we live. Thus every poem is an instance of universal ontology presented and exemplified in a logical concretion. Foster, *The New Romantics*, draws the same conclusion about Ransom, p. 144.

thetics are Richards-once-removed: ". . . things are not poetic per se, and conversely . . . nothing can be said to be intrinsically unpoetic".[15] Though this is very like Richards' attitude toward the phantom aesthetic state, Brooks does not go so far as Richards. Beauty, rather than being almost wholly affective, is for Brooks (as for Ransom) produced by a tertiary quality in the artifact. He sees that the poet does not simply "hold the mirror up to nature", that beauty is not reflected, but created:

A mirror can only reflect the poetic object placed before it. But if we are to use the term mirror at all, it is rather a distortion mirror which the poet carries, or better still, a lens with which he gives a focus to experience. At all events, the emphasis must be placed on the poet's making. In Donne's famous comparison of the lovers to a pair of compasses, the compasses are poetic in the only sense in which objects can ever be legitimately poetic – they function integrally in a poem. (page 12, *MPT*)

The movement from concern with poetic creation to poetic effect is typical of Brooks' interest. 'Function' sounds the note which is to dominate his criticism, though when he uses 'pattern' as an alternative term, there is present the same confusion between objective and affective aesthetics which has been noted in Ransom. Perhaps, after all, 'pattern' is the better word, for he is concerned primarily with the artifact: "Unless one asserts the primacy of the pattern a poem becomes merely a bouquet of intrinsically beautiful items."[16] Brooks tries to avoid the extremes of both subjectivism and objectivism by saying that despite the uniqueness of each reader's reaction to the words of a poem, the relationships which the poet indicates among the words remain constant. He is not unaware of the deficiencies of this stance:

The temper of our times is strongly relativistic. We have had impressed upon us the necessity for reading a poem in terms of its historical context, and that kind of reading has been carried on so successfully that some of us have been tempted to feel that it is the only kind of reading possible. We tend to say that every poem is an expression of its age; that we must be careful to ask of it only what its own age asked; that we must judge it only by the canons of its age. Any attempt to view it *sub specie aeternitatis*, we feel, must result in illusion.

Perhaps it must. Yet, if poetry exists as poetry in any meaningful sense, the attempt must be made. (x-xi, *WWU*)

---

[15] Cleanth Brooks, *Modern Poetry and the Tradition* (Chapel Hill, 1939), p. 11. Future references will be included in the text. This book will be distinguished from *The Well Wrought Urn* by the initials *MPT*.
[16] Cleanth Brooks, *The Well Wrought Urn*, distinguished in future references by the initials *WWU*, p. 164.

The attitude that every poem is, in some degree, contemporary is characteristic of the new critics. A poem must exist as a timeless aesthetic experience as well as a document of its age. "If the wordplay is once effective and justified, then it is always justified – regardless of the period in which the play was produced" (page 28, *MPT*). Ultimately this is true, for an understanding of historical considerations may be incorporated into the reader's sensibility and thus become timeless in much the same way as the poem is timeless.

Brooks, like Ransom, sees the poem as partly self-creating. The poet does not, in the composition of a poem, record an experience, he undergoes an experience: "The experience he 'communicates' is itself created by the organization of the symbols which he uses. The total poem is therefore the communication, and indistinguishable from it" (page 59, *MPT*). But Brooks differs from Ransom in insisting upon the essential unity of all the elements in a poem. The poet's task is "to unify experience". And the poem, "if it be a true poem, is a simulacrum of reality – in this sense, at least, it is an 'imitation' – by *being* an experience rather than any mere statement about experience or any mere abstraction from experience" (pages 212-213, *WWU*). This, in less metaphysical terms, we have already met in Richards. Brooks' heritage is here very clear, and it also includes Empson. Brooks says that to be an experience, the poem must be experienced by someone, and for that experience to have the unity which the poet intended, the reader must do a great deal. Too often the reader places the task wholly in the poet's hands "when he ought to be assuming the burden of proof himself" (page 76, *WWU*).

The failure to realize that a poem is an experience causes the critic to talk nonsense:

Most of our difficulties in criticism are rooted in the heresy of paraphrase. If we allow ourselves to be misled by it, we distort the relation of the poem to its "truth," we raise the problem of belief in a vicious and crippling form, we split the poem between its "form" and its "content" – we bring the statement to be conveyed into an unreal competition with science or philosophy or theology. (page 201, *WWU*)

Pushed to its extreme, this attitude makes criticism impossible, and as critics "we emerge with nothing more enlightening than this graceless bit of tautology: the poem says what the poem says" (page 74, *WWU*). The warnings concerned with the heresy of paraphrase are rather like the warnings concerning cancer on cigarette packs. No one is likely to question their validity, but neither smoking nor criticism is likely to be abolished. Since Brooks' greatest skill is in his particular kind of paraphrase, he does not himself pursue his warning to the logical conclusion. Since paraphrase is preliminary to analysis, it is impossible to have New Criticism without it. The alternatives are impressionism and historical scholarship. So long as paraphrase is a tool, not an end, it serves a very necessary function. It is against the abuse of paraphrase that Brooks warns.

It seems to me that Brooks might have profited from a fuller incorporation of Richards' distinctions between objective and subjective. Though they by no means provide all the answers, these distinctions allow the critic to realize his situation more fully than do Brooks' attempts to treat objective and subjective simultaneously. In "Appendix 2" of *The Well Wrought Urn*, Brooks faces the problem for a moment and then turns his attention from theory to practice, from essence to function:

No theory of poetry can make poetry autonomous in the sense that it denies that every poem is rooted in language and in the language of a particular time. We *start* outside the poem. But there is another sense in which it may be held that we are forced to *go outside the poem*: in determining the power of the tensions generated, the fact of the reconciliations achieved, etc., the reader will have to have recourse to his own experience, and on occasion different readers may disagree. What will appear sentimental to one reader may appear, to another, to be a legitimate reconciliation. Again no theory of criticism can do away with the subjective element (though the consequences of this ineradicable subjectivity are easily exaggerated). Yet it seems to me that there is a real gain in attempting to judge a poem in terms of its characteristic structure, a dramatic structure, rather than in attempting to abstract propositions from the poem and to measure them by canons of scientific or philosophic truth. (page 255, *WWU*)

Brooks has destroyed his straw man, but it may be wondered if it is not easier to underestimate the fallacy of subjective statistic than to overestimate it, for where Empson and Brooks are most at fault (in analysis rather than theory), the source of the problem is often a mistaking of purely personal associations for associations generally available to the reader of poetry.[17]

In the first appendix to *The Well Wrought Urn*, Brooks sets criteria

[17]　In saying this, I am guilty of the same fault: assuming that I know what is generally available to the reader, but such an instance as Empson's admitted overreading of 'ruined choirs' as the monasteries destroyed by Henry VIII ("Note for the Third Edition", *Seven Types of Ambiguity*, p. xviii) is not wholly atypical. The readings of Crashaw (pp. 250-253) would also seem to fall outside the 'normal' reader's scope.

for poetry of the most effective kind: "functional imagery, irony, and complexity of attitude" (page 231, *WWU*). The danger in such criteria is that they exclude as inferior poems which operate by diffuseness or heterogeneity. And there is a second, opposite, danger against which Ransom has warned: it is possible to find ambiguity, rather than heterogeneity, at almost any point one chooses to look. And a reader who is busy inventing meaningful ambiguities is in danger of losing sight of the larger structures of the poem. Although Ransom's objections to Empson's readings are generally applicable to the readings of Brooks, Brooks' more single-minded attention to matters of structure serves as a corrective to a possible overinventiveness as a reader. Two readings from Shakespeare, one by Empson, the other by Brooks, indicate just how close are the methods of the two critics: the 'bare ruined choirs'[18] and the 'daggers breeched in gore'[19] might exchange commentators almost unnoticed.

Cleanth Brooks shares the view of the complexity of life which has been noted in the previous critics, and he agrees that poetry must therefore be complex if it is to be true: "There are nuances of attitude that can be given in no other way than by the aid of the qualification which the metaphor or simile produces" (page 30, *MPT*). Like Hulme, he sees that "plain speech is essentially inaccurate", and like Hulme, he seeks accuracy through concrete, not abstract, combinations. And because "nearly all mature attitudes represent some sort of mingling of the approbative and the satirical" (page 29, *MPT*), meaningful ambiguity must be the essential device of all poetry which is of the first rank.

Such is the basis for his preference for modern, Jacobean, and Elizabethan poetry. The three ages see that "the poet, the imaginative man, has his particular value in his superior power to reconcile the irrelevant or apparently warring elements of experience" (page 33, *MPT*). On the other hand, the early eighteenth century wrote poetry on an assumption which is radically false:

The prime mistake of the neoclassic period, then, was not that it gave vent to the satiric impulse but rather that it segregated it from other impulses, leaving its tragedy too noble and too easily didactic; or, on the other hand, when it attempted to stir the heartstrings, too sentimental. Neoclassical love poetry is too exclusively love poetry; neoclassic satire, too narrowly satiric. (page 230, *MPT*)

---

[18] William Empson, *Seven Types of Ambiguity*, pp. 5 ff.
[19] Brooks, *The Well Wrought Urn*, pp. 22 ff.

Brooks' classic essay on *The Rape of the Lock*[20] makes Pope, by this definition, not a neoclassical poet. And Samuel Monk's essay on the madness of Lemuel Gulliver[21] proves the same of Swift. A definition of neoclassicism which excludes both Pope and Swift is suspect. But, at any rate, the distinction which Brooks is seeking is between poetry of inclusion and poetry of exclusion.

Eliot's method is, says Brooks, the antithesis of the neoclassical method:

The basic method used in *The Waste Land* may be described as the application of the principle of complexity. The poet works in terms of surface parallelisms which in reality make ironical contrasts, and in terms of surface contrasts which in reality constitute parallelisms .... The two aspects taken together give the effect of chaotic experience ordered into a new whole, though the realistic surface of experience is not violated by the apparent forcing upon it of a predetermined scheme. (page 167, *MPT*)

Here Brooks' unwillingness to give full credit to the subjective-objective division of poetry vitiates a useful observation. Although he appears to be saying that Eliot's method is antithetical to Ransom's idea of warring structure and texture, Brooks' system amounts to almost the same thing. Both critics imply that, subjectively, any group of objects or ideas may be said to have unity – the unity of simultaneous perception – in that they are unified by simultaneity in the reader's consciousness. Objectively, in order to have unity there must be rational, cognitive, relationships which are based on similarities among the objects themselves. Thus it is possible to have an 'experiential' unity or a 'cognitive' unity. All cognitive unity is reinforced by the prior experiential unity, but the converse need not be true. The reader must construct a unity in order to experience the unity of the poem, and the poet must present objects in such a way that cognition can aid in that construction.

Brooks suggests that the method which he admires in Eliot is universal, though there are degrees of complexity:

The essential structure of a poem (as distinguished from rational or logical structure of the "statement" which we abstract from it) resembles that of architecture or painting: it is a pattern of resolved stresses. Or to move closer still to poetry by considering the temporal arts, the structure of a poem resembles that of a ballet or musical composition. It is a pattern of resolutions and balances and harmonizations, developed though a temporal scheme. (page 203, *WWU*)

[20] *The Well Wrought Urn*, pp. 80 ff.
[21] Samuel Holt Monk, "The Pride of Lemuel Gulliver", *Sewanee Review* (Winter, 1955), 48-71.

The implied bow to Richards makes Brooks' notion of the heresy of paraphrase clearer. We destroy the poem any time we translate it from the language of poetry to the language of science: all prose statements must represent a movement in that direction. So stated, the profundity disappears, and 'heresy' seems too pretentious a term.

The perception which Brooks has of life requires that irony and paradox (he uses the terms interchangeably) be at the heart of 'mature' poetry:

Irony is the most general term that we have for the kind of qualification which the various elements in a context receive from the context . . . . Moreover, irony is our most general term for indicating that recognition of incongruities – which, again, pervades all poetry to a degree far beyond what our conventional criticism has been heretofore willing to allow. (pages 209-210)

It would appear that for Brooks, irony (the juxtaposition of conflicting elements) is the tertiary quality which can be perceived as the beauty of a poem, for it is through irony that the poet achieves unity in complexity.[22] Paradox is the means by which most of the essential truths must be stated if they are to be stated at all: "most of the language of lovers is such . . . so is most of the language of religion. . . . Indeed, almost any insight important enough to warrant a great poem apparently has to be stated in such terms" (pages 17-18, *WWU*). Ransom objects that this claim is extravagant. Cognitive unity is not a universal quality of great poetry, though of course any respectable Empsonian can supply cognitive paradox for any juxtaposition. We may note Brooks once more refusing the services of the subjective-objective dichotomy and then proceed to his specific statements as to the nature of metaphor:

The dramatization [of a poetic experience] demands that the antithetical aspects of memory be coalesced into one entity which – if we take it on the level of statement – is a paradox, the assertion of the union of opposites. (page 213, *WWU*)

Brooks uses 'structure' in his discussions of metaphor, but it is not the same structure which we have met in Ransom's work. By structure Ransom means form – whether that form be of meter, or idea, or deno-

---

[22] It is interesting to see Brooks present Ransom's condemnation of the source of this idea in Richards without acknowledging his own advocacy of it. See Wimsatt and Brooks, *Literary Criticism: A Short History* (New York, 1964), pp. 620-621.

tation. Brooks means something broader; at times he almost seems to mean 'poem':

The structure meant is a structure of meanings, evaluations, and interpretations; and the principle of unity which informs it seems to be one of balancing and harmonizing connotations, attitudes, and meanings. But even here one needs to make important qualifications; the principle is not one which involves the arrangement of the various elements into homogeneous groupings, pairing like with like. It unites the like with the unlike. It does not unite them, however, by the simple process of allowing one connotation to cancel out another nor does it reduce the contradictory attitudes to harmony by a process of substraction. The unity is not a unity of the sort to be achieved by the reduction and simplification appropriate to an algebraic formula. It is a positive unity, not a negative; it represents not a residue but an achieved harmony. (page 195, *WWU*)

This passage might have been written by Richards (in which case he would have spoken of the poetry of inclusion), or by Tate (he would have called such poetry 'tensive'), or by Empson (such poetry is ambiguity of the seventh type). Brooks, like Ransom, acknowledges 'meanderings' which have a positive function (page 209, *WWU*) and what he calls 'the principle of rich indirection' (page 73, *WWU*), but he insists on a unity within the poem – among the materials of the poem – and so does not accept Ransom's idea of heterogeneity.

"The essence of poetry is metaphor", Brooks tells us, and since he has asserted that the essence of poetry is irony/paradox, it is clear that metaphor must involve the qualities of unified opposition which he attributes to irony (page 248, *WWU*). He agrees with Hulme that metaphor is necessary because "it is through the production of energetic metaphor, or live 'myths' that the poet attempts to break through the pattern of 'abstract experience' and give man a picture of himself as man" (pages 101-102, *MPT*). The various metaphors within a poem 'function' by providing a window to the nature of man:

The value of the figure must in all cases be referred to its function in the context in which it occurs, with the recognition that the range of possible function is wide; the figure may have a negative function as well as a positive – may serve irony as well as ennoblement. Our only test for the validity of any figure must be an appeal to the whole context in which it occurs: Does it contribute to the total effect, or not? (page 15, *MPT*)

Of course it "contributes to the total effect"; everything and anything present at a particular time to a particular intelligence produces a total effect. Clearly Brooks is not saying just what he means. Though it risks the heresy of paraphrase, the passage may be restated something like this: Any object can serve as material for poetry; the only requirement is that all of the objects present in a single poem be such that they can be organized (despite and because of their contrariness) into a unity – that unity is the unity of a single, complex experience, and it need not be the result of the likenesses in the elements which make up the poem. In the first appendix to *The Well Wrought Urn* Brooks seems to be approaching such a statement:

The essence of poetry is metaphor, and metaphor is finally analogical rather than logical. The presence or absence of strict logic, therefore, has no *direct* relation to the kind of coherency to which good poetry aspires, and without which it cannot be "good." (page 248)

It is not difficult to see reasons for Brooks' preference for metaphysical poetry. Not only is the imagery of metaphysical poetry full of irony and paradox, but:

the metaphysical poets reveal the essentially functional character of all metaphor. We cannot remove the comparisons from their poems, as we might remove ornaments or illustrations attached to a statement, without demolishing the poems. The comparison *is* the poem in a structural sense. (page 15, *MPT*)

The best of Brooks' readings are the illustrations which he gives of this principle. In two essays which have become models of explication ("The Naked Babe and the Cloak of Manliness" and "Keats' Sylvan Historian")[23] he indicates the possible associational perceptions in the varied materials of *Macbeth* and "Ode on a Grecian Urn" which have since come to seem part of the poems. Brooks' contributions, like Empsons', are largely in his readings of specific passages. The elements of his theories we have met in critics previously discussed, though not with quite the same set of emphases.

The most useful thing which Brooks contributes to a theory of metaphor is the development which he makes in Richards' 'poetry of exclusion'. He suggests that such a division might be developed "into a kind of scale for determining the value of poetry":

Low in the scale one would find a rather simple poetry in which the associations of the various elements that go to make up the poem are similar in tone and therefore can be unified under one rather simple attitude – poems of simple affection, positive, "external" satires, etc. Higher in the scale, one would find poems in which the variety and clash among the elements to be comprehended under a total attitude are sharper. In tragedy, where the clash is at its sharpest – where the tension between attraction and repulsion is

---

[23]   Both are included in *The Well Wrought Urn*.

most powerful – one would probably find the highest point in the scale.
So much for the positive side; but there is a negative side too, where one
would place those poems which failed to secure unity at all – or achieved
only a specious reconciliation of attitudes – the sentimental poem. (pages
256-257, *WWU*)

If we substitute 'metaphor' for 'poem' in this passage, we get a notion
of a range from 'positive' to 'negative' metaphor, which though based
upon affective phenomena, gives a means of discriminating in a useful
manner among the effects of metaphor. Brooks' negative scale does not
hold up; the poem which presents unfused elements is at the opposite
extreme from that which is sentimental. Brooks' theory does not admit
poems which present, rather than fuse – which suggest acceptance
rather than unification. It is possible, however, for poetry to avoid the
Eleatic flaw. Consider:

> Wild boars and all
> Are blown along with it;
> Storm wind of fall.[24]

These lines demand acceptance, not unification. A very powerful effect
can be achieved by presenting materials which demand not a working
out of cognitive relationships, but an acceptance of the absence of such
relations.

In the essay "Metaphysical Poetry and Propaganda Art", Brooks
moves further toward a theory of what I have called 'negative metaphor'; unfortunately his demand that all poetry, if it is 'good', possess
a degree of 'irony' and 'paradox' makes it necessary for him to label
'positive metaphor' inferior. Of course if positive metaphor is judged by
the standards of negative metaphor it must seem a very poor thing.
Brooks has reversed Johnson's position. Johnson judged negative metaphor by the standards of positive metaphor and found it wanting.
Brooks recognizes the importance of negative metaphor, that it is the
basic device of metaphysical poetry, but he also denies the value of
metaphor which is positive:

It will be easy to illustrate this general principle of metaphysical poetry from
its use of metaphor. Any comparison has in it an essential incongruity, even
the most trite comparison. Eyes are not really very much like stars, nor love
like a red, red rose. The poet who is at the mercy of a narrow decorum,
logical or scientific, is apt to depend too much on the likeness existing between the objects he compares. He lets no recognition of these disparities

---

[24] Bashō, "The Autumn Storm", *An Introduction to Haiku*, ed. Harold G.
Henderson (New York, 1958), p. 34.

appear in the poem. Consequently, the fault of timid metaphor is that it does not wear well. On a first reading it may seem plausible. Closer acquaintance, however, reveals the disparities, and a shift of the poem into an ironic context reveals them cruelly. The metaphysical conceit represents a complete reversal of this situation. The disparities are recognized and deliberately exploited by the poet; they are gathered up into the context of the poem. Since the destructive elements are contained within the comparison, the conceit, if unsuccessful, rather than wearing out, explodes from within. If it does not explode with a first reading, it is extremely durable. There are no further ludicrous disparities to be revealed on later readings. (pages 44-45, *MPT*)

Hulme and Richards suggest that 'positive' metaphors are the result of familiarity, rather than newness, and that any metaphor may become positive to the point of losing its identity as metaphor if it is used often enough and if the use is careless. Their position is more convincing than that of Brooks. Still, Brooks' ideas are far more satisfactory than the Johnsonian violent yoking; Brooks' additions and corrections to Richards' theories, though they sometimes throw out the baby with the bathwater, are worthwhile.

III

GRANDSONS AND GENEOLOGISTS: W. K. WIMSATT, Jr., PHILIP WHEELWRIGHT, MURRAY KRIEGER

> A literary work of art is a complex of detail (an arti-
> fact, if we may be allowed that metaphor for what is
> only a verbal object), a composition so complicated of
> human values that its interpretation is dictated by the
> understanding of it, and so complicated as to seem in
> the highest degree individual – a concrete universal.
> *The Verbal Icon*

A. THE FALLACIES OF W. K. WIMSATT

Although *The Verbal Icon: Studies in the Meaning of Poetry*[1] is but one of the many attempts to synthesize and correct the accomplishments of twentieth century criticism, it is provocative for one who seeks to discover in the work of New Critics some workable sense of 'metaphor' as a tool for understanding the nature and function of poetry. It is quite derivative, and the relationships which exist between Wimsatt and the critics discussed above are easy to perceive. If a rough distinction is made between Richards as a theoretician and Empson as a reader, it is obvious that Wimsatt here belongs with Richards. There is little in *The Verbal Icon* of the close analysis of specific lines which makes up *Seven Types of Ambiguity* and which dominates *The Well Wrought Urn*. Yet, Wimsatt writes with a more obvious dependence upon previous critics than does Richards. His work is kin to Ransom's *The New Criticism* and to Brooks' *Modern Poetry and the Tradition*, but it is less original than either. Like the other books to be considered in this chapter, *The Verbal Icon* is a book of perfection, not of innovation. Like Ransom and Brooks, Wimsatt begins with a correction for the New Criticism; he wishes to search out the particular biases which vitiate the value and impede the progress of criticism.

---

[1] W. K. Wimsatt, Jr. and Monroe C. Beardsley, *The Verbal Icon: Studies in the Meaning of Poetry* (Lexington, Kentucky, 1954). Future references will be included in the text.

Two of the tendencies which he isolates are of particular interest for the present study, one because it indicates his kinship with Richards, the other because it represents the rebellion against Richards which has been noted in the work of Ransom and Brooks, and to a lesser extent in the criticism of Allen Tate. Wimsatt, like Richards, warns of the danger of the 'Intentional Fallacy'. And he is at one with Ransom and Brooks in seeing the futility of searching for the meaning of the poem in the mind of the poet. He realizes that to seek the moment of poetic inspiration as the definition of poetry is to compound the subjective fallacy to no worthy end:

A poem does not come into existence by accident. The words of a poem, as Professor Stoll has remarked, come out of a head, not out of a hat. Yet to insist on the designing intellect as a *cause* of a poem is not to grant the design or intention as a *standard* by which the critic is to judge the worth of the poet's performance. (page 4)

Even if the intention were granted as the standard, facts about that intention are, most often, not available – and when available wonderfully irrelevant.[2] Wimsatt sees the result of a search for intention as a desertion of the poem for the poet. He invents a straw-critic who illustrates the absurdity of the intentional fallacy. Such a critic exclaims:

"I am not interested in technique for itself: it is either petty precision or exaggerated, even unnatural, figures of speech. The only thing that can justify technique (or palliate its outrages) is the lofty genius, the thoughts and passions of the great poet."

Certainly no complete critic is "interested in technique for itself", and it may be argued that Wimsatt has made his critic speak in too foolish a fashion to represent fairly the virtues of 'intentional' criticism, but there is agreement among our critics that the poet's intention is neither clearly formulated prior to composition, nor is it available to the critic. Thus, the poem must to some degree be considered *sub specie aeternitatis*; attempts to reconstruct the specific *milieu* of the poem may be both interesting and useful, but they cannot be conclusive.

The second point of interest in Wimsatt's book is his discussion of the obverse of the intentional fallacy. The affective fallacy gathers coherently the objections which the second generation of New Critics has to Richards. Whereas the intentional critic deserted the poem for the poet, the affective critic deserts the poem for the reader. Wimsatt's affective critic exclaims:

[2]   Frost's comments on "Stopping by Woods on a Snowy Evening" are a classic case in point.

"Don't talk to me about technical features (rhyme or figures) or about the parts of poems. They are justified only as they help to elicit from the audience its total unique response, which *is* the value of the poem." (Intro., pages xvii-xviii)

In the extreme case such a critic produces only the worst form of impressionistic criticism: criticism which is wholly personal and couched in terms of physiological reactions or personal associations. Again objections may be raised: such extreme impressionism need not result, and the critic who denies the importance of 'the total unique response' of the reader risks being little more than a technician. The affective critic may be guilty of a less compounded form of subjectivism than the intentional critic, yet Wimsatt is right in warning against both extremes of impressionism: historical and affective. The two, he says, are really parts of the same thing, and therefore they have a single cause: "The intentional and affective fallacies have frequently come about through a critic's distaste for problems of technique, and . . . a sound view of technique and its relation to . . . 'content' will come close to ensuring avoidance of the psychological fallacies" (Intro., page xvii).

If the pure positions which Wimsatt ascribes to the intentional and affective critics are maintained, there remains but one other possibility: the poem itself. If a coinage in the manner of Wimsatt is attempted, critics who concentrate only upon 'the poem', may be accused of the 'artifactual fallacy'. And if such a position is written in straw, the artifactual critic cries: "Do not speak to me of the cause or the result of a poem. The important thing is its essence, not its source or its function. Nothing is important except the poem itself – a poem should not mean but be." There is, of course, truth in the position of this 'pure' artifactual critic: the poem must be the critic's main concern, and the composition of the reader's breakfast or the poet's childhood must be irrelevant to the kind of aesthetic experience about which the critic can speak other than nonsense. But as the analysis of Richards' triangle of perception presented in Chapter One, above, suggests, the 'poem itself' does not exist in any significant way if it is divorced from both poet and reader.

It would seem that criticism is faced with a dilemma: what is it that forms the matter upon which the critic operates? What is a poem, and where does it exist? The affective critic places it within his own mind or in the mind of an imagined reader and so reduces it to almost total subjectivity. The intentional critic compounds this subjectivity by placing the poem in the mind of the poet, who is removed from the

critic and reader by time, space, and experience. At its extreme, artifactual criticism reduces the poem to a series of marks on a page and
so denies communication and with communication, judgment. Clearly,
each of the three positions in its purity makes criticism impossible. But
of course there is no aesthetic law which demands that the critic, set in
a world of contradiction, compromise, and ambiguity must reduce his
position to the absolute or vanish. The problem, it would seem, is to
determine just what combination of the three possible positions is most
satisfactory, given modern interests and mortal limitations. Wimsatt
attempts an answer, and aside from rhetorical absolutes, his position is
strikingly like that which Richards presents in *Coleridge on Imagination*
and *The Philosophy of Rhetoric*.

Wimsatt notes "the two main and perennially opposed axes of literary
theory, the cognitive and the affective, the axis of order or being against
chaos or nothing" (page 272), but he prefers to the 'metaphysical'
criticism of Ransom and Winters the "far more congenial and influen-
tial . . . psychological view of I. A. Richards, that poetry is harmony of
impulses, and . . . the middle view of T. S. Eliot, that poetry is verbal
formula or objective correlative of emotions" (page 272). Despite his
distaste for the affective fallacy, he finds in

the emphasis upon impulses that are only "incipient" or "imaginal" and
upon the equilibrium of these . . . a clause in the system of Richards which
corresponds to the detachment or disinterest of other systems [which] performs the same function of setting off aesthetic from other values. The
Richardsian criticism, by dwelling upon patterns and harmony of responses,
has, in fact accomplished something very much like a reconciliation of
earlier and cruder theories of order and being. (page 272)

Wimsatt thus sees one of the major flaws in Richards' theories as self-
correcting, and when he asserts that "art is neither merely subjective,
nor merely objective", he is at one with the Richards of *Coleridge on
Imagination*. Like Richards, Wimsatt is aware that to speak of a poem
as an artifact is false, "but the same disability for criticism inheres in
all logical formulas" (page 151). And like the Richards of *The Philosophy of Rhetoric*, he realizes that criticism must speak of the poem as
artifact in spite of the fallacy:

I am interested in maintaining no more than that the concept of specific
substance, as it may help to map many simpler provinces of descriptive
technique, distinguishing the style of Swift, for example, from that of
Johnson and that of Keats, is also a concept through which some insight
may be had into the more dimly lit mirror relations of the realm of metaphor. (page 151)

But Wimsatt is not content to rest with the idea that we speak of the poem as artifact only for convenience: "Expressiveness asks for stylization and surpasses mere imitation of natural proportions. A work of art is recognized by the necessity of its inner form – the uniqueness of its rhythm" (page 124). This moves from Richards towards Brooks. Such a piling up of metaphors in prose is likely to cause a confusion of tenors and vehicles. I suspect that it is responsible for Wimsatt's assertion of the existence of 'the verbal icon' – an idea which on its face seems a contradiction in terms:

> The term *icon* is used today by semiotic writers to refer to a verbal sign which somehow shares the properties of, or resembles, the objects which it denotes. The same term in its more usual meaning refers to a visual image and especially to one which is a religious symbol. The verbal image which most fully realizes its verbal capacities is that which is not merely a bright picture (in the usual modern meaning of the term *image*) but also is an interpretation of reality in its metaphoric and symbolic dimensions. Thus: *The Verbal Icon*. (Prefatory note, no pagination)

In theory, a verbal icon is just what both poetry and criticism need. There would be no confusion as to what a poem meant, no problem in realizing the total aesthetic experience of the poem. And since such an entity would be both external object and engram, criticism would completely avoid both the artifactual and the affective fallacies. But it may be doubted that such a hybrid exists; certainly Wimsatt gives no examples.

About the best that can be done is to suggest that the notion of icon is literally inappropriate to verbal art. If it is to be used at all, it should perhaps refer not to the external element of poetry, but to the response which the perceiver of art has to an engram which shares in some measure the qualities of those non-verbal objects which we call icons. The more usual word for such an engram-response complex is symbol.

In his discussion of the Chicago Critics[3] Wimsatt is aware of the disparity between 'thing' and 'poem', but he pleads expediency:

> For if anything about poetry is clear at all it is that a poem is not really a thing, like a horse or a house, but only *analogically* so. The analogy I would maintain is a good one, highly instructive, and no doubt the only way by which criticism of a poem (rather than talk about its author and its audience or about its message) can be conducted. But at the same time, a poem is, if it is anything at all, a verbal discourse . . . . hence it is a human act, physical and mental. The only "thing" is the poet speaking. To treat this act of

[3] Wimsatt, "The Chicago Critics: The Fallacy of the Neo-Classical Species", *The Verbal Icon*, pp. 41-65.

thought, feeling, and verbal expression not just in its psychological causes nor in its effects on hearers, nor yet in its abstract logical existence as communicable ideas merely, but precisely as a kind of solid "thing," an objectification of thought and feeling in verbal expression, is a requisite for critical thinking. This much one has to insist upon. But that is a long way from making the criticism of the poem "literal" or "scientific" in any privileged sense. (page 50)

This passage is particularly revealing, for here Wimsatt faces the same impasse noted above in Richards and Ransom and Brooks. The New Critic is essentially an affectivist making do with objective terms. Or to put it another way, the New Critic realizes that poetry is made up of stimulus and response, that response is by far the most important element, but that it is to the nature of the stimulus that he must turn his attention if he is to say anything about poetry which will be of value to other readers. The artifactual elements of the poem function as an objective correlative, and although the correlation is between affective states, it is the 'object' which is available for comment. Though this is a too facile solution of the problems which Wimsatt is trying to face, I think the direction is a true one. Wimsatt's clearest statement of this idea is, after all, not very clear:

Poetry is characteristically a discourse about both emotions and objects, or about the emotive quality of objects. The emotions correlative to the objects of poetry become a part of the matter dealt with — not communicated to the reader like an infection or disease, not inflicted mechanically like a bullet or knife wound, not administered like a poison, not simply expressed as expletives or grimaces or rhythms, but presented in their objects and contemplated as a pattern of knowledge. Poetry is a way of fixing emotions or making them more permanently perceptible when objects have undergone a functional change from culture to culture, or when as simple facts of history they have lost emotive value with loss of immediacy. (page 38)

Ultimately, Wimsatt admits that "the being which is now set up as the center of poetic interest is conscious or internal man himself, rather than man or any part of his environment as externally reportable or imitable" (page 272). This is, of course, just Richards' position in *The Philosophy of Rhetoric*.

If the relationship between engram and icon is thus granted, it is possible to see something of the nature of icon by its actions in poetic discourse:

Iconicity enforces disparity. The symbol has more substance than a non-iconic symbol and hence is more clearly realized as a thing separate from its referents and as one of the productions of our own spirit. Seeing a work of art, says Ortega y Gasset, is seeing the window pane with the garden pasted behind it, or the world inverted into the belvedere of our concepts. (page 217)

The purpose of the icon, it seems, is to create an extra vigilance in the reader, to make the elements of his being, his engrams, more readily available to his conscious mind than is customary. And the belvedere of the icon functions something like a Claude Lorrain glass – the reader is not only more aware of engrams, but he is enabled to organize them in ways before unavailable.

The structure which results from the 'iconicity' of poetry, Wimsatt calls 'The Concrete Universal'. And he notes the long tradition of such an idea: Edward Young, Johnson, Hegel, Coleridge, Mill, Tate, and Ransom.[4] "Character", he says, "is one type of concrete universal; but there are other types, as many perhaps as the central terms of criticism; but most can be learned, I believe, by examination of metaphor – the structure most characteristic of concentrated poetry" (page 79). His general idea of metaphor is that which I have attributed to Richards: "behind a metaphor lies a resemblance between two classes, and hence a more general third class. This class is unnamed and most likely remains unnamed and is apprehended only through the metaphor" (page 79). Here we have the idea of a third thing – of one thing for two – which can be perceived only through the superimposition of tenor and vehicle. But this third entity is not achieved at the expense of the other two, "for words which are fused into a poem have their new value not by losing their first or ordinary meanings but only by retaining these" (page 130). Wimsatt has the same notion of the accuracy of metaphor which has been noted in Hulme. It is not only "the principle of all poetry but . . . also inevitable in practical criticism and . . . present in proportion as criticism moves beyond the historical report or the academic exercise" (page 49). "Plain speech is essentially inaccurate."

The notion of metaphor as a 'war-embrace', which each of our critics has granted in some degree, is shared by Wimsatt: "It would appear to me that recent criticism has made out a strong case indeed for some kind of paradoxical tension as an intrinsic character, or mainspring, of most if not all poetry" (page 274). But Wimsatt, like Brooks on occasion, demands a holism; in so doing he seems at times to deny the possibility of "'abstract' or 'nonrepresentational' art. . . . Nonrepresenta-

---

[4] John Crowe Ransom, *Kenyon Review*, XVI (1954), 554-564, discusses 'Concrete Universal' in terms of Hegel and those whom Hegel influenced.

tional of what? Red is like a sunset, an oval is like an egg or something like an egg. No visible thing is so unlike all else that it is invincibly a symbol of nothing" (page 137). This is Empson's method. And Wimsatt, like Empson, is unwilling to grant 'experiential' unity; rather he insists that the relationship which accounts for unity must be within the object:

If objects are ever connected by "emotional congruity," as in the association psychology which J. S. Mill inherited from the eighteenth century, this can mean only that similar emotions attach to various objects because of similarity in the object or in their relations. What makes one angry is something false, insulting, or unjust. What makes one afraid is a cyclone, a mob, a holdup man. And in each case the emotion is somewhat different. (page 27)

The last half of this statement goes a long way toward denying the first half. In his eagerness to destroy the affective fallacy, Wimsatt throws away the initiating force of emotion – the differences in a work of art which result from differences in its perceiver. There is a certain kind of unity imposed upon objects by simultaneity – regardless of the degree of cognitive similarity. And there are infinite degrees of unity between the purely cognitive and the purely experiential. When he is not arguing a case by destroying strawmen, Wimsatt is aware of this distinction. It is possible, he says, to have a unity, "an abstraction which is the effect not wholly of the metaphor elaborated logically (in a metaphysical way) but of a working on two axes, by association rather than by logic, by a three-dimensional complexity of structure" (page 80). Such a division (between experiential and cognitive unity) provides a system in which it is possible to make use of both affective and objective aesthetics, and though Wimsatt repeatedly approaches such a division, his critical vocabulary is finally Eleatic:

A literary work of art is a complex of detail (an artifact, if we may be allowed that metaphor for what is only a verbal object), a composition so complicated of human values that its interpretation is dictated by the understanding of it, and so complicated as to seem in the highest degree individual – a concrete universal. (page 77)

Wimsatt's debt to Richards is very clear. The critic MUST use objective terms, but he MUST NOT forget that he speaks of affective phenomena.

Wimsatt presents as 'one of the most precise attempts to define metaphor' the work of W. B. Stanford in *Greek Metaphor*.[5] Stanford suggests that a metaphor is a '*stereoscope of ideas*', and this term, with the Coleridgeian 'war-embrace', provides a basis for the kinship in the theories of metaphor discussed thus far. Like the earlier New Critics,

[5]   Stanford, *Greek Metaphor*.

Wimsatt finds the seventeenth-century metaphysicals to be the best exemplars of such an idea of metaphor:

Given the condition that the metaphysical poet was to deal in simple species of objects, as he found them named in the dictionary or treatise, the source of his originality and individuation had to lie in the relations he was able to set up between objects. This is another way of getting at the celebrated *discordia concors*, the ontological distance between the objects which the metaphysical poet yoked by violence together. Originality of relation is distance. And a kind of circuity of dependencies is completed if we observe that when objects are pulled from such distances so violently together, a certain firmness in their naming is requisite if they are to survive as objects, not be melted or dissipated – or to change the figure, if the focus of one upon the other is to remain intelligible . . . . For with concreteness of substance relationship is multiply invited. With the concreteness of metaphor, predication is solid or indefinite, and meditation limitless. (pages 150-151)

In such poetry not only the number and quality of associations which can be established among the discordant elements is significant, but also the maintenance of the individuality of each of the terms. Wimsatt calls metaphor the 'confrontation and mutual reflection of objects' (page 148), and he realizes that there is a tendency to concentrate on the reflection rather than the confrontation.

Romantic poetry in particular, says Wimsatt, insists on the similarity; "In such a structure again the element of tension in disparity is not so important as for metaphysical wit. The interest derives not from our being aware of disparity where likeness is firmly insisted on, but in an opposite activity of discerning the design which is latent in the multi-form sensuous picture" (page 110). In such poetry the typical metaphor is positive; that is, it relies on the reader to perceive likeness in the face of disparity, and to mute those elements of meaning which force the tenor and vehicle apart. Such a system is closely related to the idea of decorum. The attention of the reader is expected to remain upon a relatively few, conventional sets of associations. "Pictorial notes might be gorgeous or even lavish, but they tended to be typical. That in fact was the point. Even concreteness had to stay within lines" (page 142). The danger of employing such metaphors is that they so soon die. Poetry which relies on positive metaphor very soon becomes cliché. The Petrarchan sonnets of the English Renaissance, the grave-yard poetry of the eighteenth century, and the pathetic fallacies of the nineteenth-century romantics are cases in point.

Disparity of tenor and vehicle is so important to metaphor that Wimsatt suggests that a difference in class is essential:

A certain traitor is like Judas; a certain tyrant is like Caesar. The two ideas of the analogy belong in the same specific class. But when a man is called a skunk, specific difference as well as similarity is involved, the predication is concrete, there is metaphor. (page 149)

Like everyone else, Wimsatt has a go at Donne's compass image; he uses it as an instance of the successful operation of negative metaphor:

The kind of similarity and the kind of disparity that ordinarily obtains between a drawing compass and a pair of parting lovers are things to be attentively considered in reading this image. And the disparity between living lovers and stiff metal is not least important to the tone of precision, restraint, and conviction which is the triumph of the poem to convey. (page 104)

It might be suggested that had Donne expressed the comparison as a metaphor, rather than as a simile, Wimsatt's point would be even better taken. The compass image, like many of Donne's conceits, begins as a simile but in its elaboration becomes a metaphor. The strategy is clear: the violence of the comparison is muted until Donne has a chance to account for discrepancies in a manner which will be aesthetically believable.

Throughout *The Verbal Icon*, Wimsatt insists that the proper level of poetry is the specific – that metaphors which are effective are those which compare one thing to another (page 149), and yet he is aware of the dangers of specificity: "we may observe that this is the level of presentation at which we encounter not only the dismal schoolbook instance of particularity but such opaque pictorial fallacies as the slice of life and local color, the irrelevant reportage of amateur short-story writers, the meticulous chunking of coffee cups one encounters in early sound movies" (page 139).

Wimsatt is unusually candid in presenting his critical principles:

I am . . . a "syncretist" . . . a person who tries to reconcile the good parts of various important theories and thus to make his own theory. I believe that there are three main poles of literary theory: (1) the mimetic or Aristotelian which does justice to the world of things and real values and keeps our criticism from being merely idealistic; (2) the emotive (as seen, for instance, in Richards) which does justice to human response to values and keeps criticism from talking too much about either ethics or metaphysics; (3) the expressionistic and linguistic (par excellence, the Crocean) which does justice to man's knowledge as reflexive and creative and keeps criticism from talking about poetry as a literal recording of either things or responses . . . .
I believe that these poles can be made the main points of reference for an indefinitely variable criticism of all poems. (pages 48-49)

Viewed as excesses these are, respectively, the artifactual, the affective, and the intentional fallacies. Though he pushes the second and third of these to unnecessary extremes in an attempt to warn critics off, and though he makes himself consciously guilty of the first, earlier critics provide ample justification. The dangers to him seem to be the sentimental, impressionistic critic and the critic who spends all his time searching among minutia in an attempt to discover the 'workshop of the poet's mind'. The scepticism which now prevails as to the even approximate identity of word and thing should be sufficient to keep critics from being too artifactual. It is probably in 'syncretic' criticism such as Wimsatt writes that our age is likely to find answers at least temporarily satisfactory to the problems involved in "What is metaphor?"

B. THE DIAPHOR OF PHILIP WHEELWRIGHT

W. K. Wimsatt's correction of the excesses of New Criticism provides a base upon which a New Critical theory of metaphor can be constructed. Philip Wheelwright begins that construction. *Metaphor and Reality*[6] is a book which in many ways belongs to New Criticism. Despite his tendency to mix myth, anthropology, and magic with close thinking, Wheelwright has much in common with I. A. Richards. He is fully aware of the importance of affectivism:

Because of the nutritive darkness of proto-semantic experience in which it has taken root, and also because of its aim, which is to represent and evoke something of the richness and wonder and mystery of the world, a tensive symbol will allow some degree (preferably not too much) both of obscurity and of variation in the responses of awareness that it calls forth. (page 95)

I THINK by this he means that the external poem serves as a stimulus which calls forth a response which in some ways depends for its particular nature on the condition of the responder as well as upon the nature of the stimulus. Though he does not mean by tension just what Tate does (he sees further dimensions in the causes of tension), there is enough agreement so that their terms can be interchanged without great distortion. Perhaps a major difference is that Wheelwright thinks of tension as partially affective: "the degree of actual tensiveness will of

---

[6] Philip Wheelwright, *Metaphor and Reality*. Future references will be included in the text.

course vary according to the sensitivity and disposition of the individual participant" (page 47).

As it must, the recognition of the role of affectivism in aesthetic perception demands some system of objective correlative: the two are inevitably companions. But Wheelwright adds another dimension: not only must the object correlate the perceptions of the reader and the poet, it must also be in some degree correlative of external reality:

As man gropes to express his complex nature and his sense of the complex world, he seeks or creates representational and expressive forms . . . which shall give some hint, always finally insufficient, of the turbulent moods within and the turbulent world of qualities and forces, promises and threats, outside him. His life oscillates between contrary pulls . . . and sometimes for lingering moments attains . . . visions. But if the vision is not to be escapist and a merely stubborn refusal to face things as they are, it will bear traces of the tension and problematic character of the experience that gave it birth.

Thus language that strives toward adequacy – as opposed to signs and words of practical intent or of mere habit – is characteristically tensive to some degree . . . . (page 46)

Here we find (1) the subjective-objective-affective aesthetic of Richards; (2) the Symbolic and Angelic Imaginations of Tate; (3) the ironic vision of Brooks; (4) the Structure-Texture war of Ransom, and finally, (5) the division of language into 'adequate' and 'practical' to which the New Critics subscribe.

Wheelwright extends Richards' division of language into the language of science and the language of poetry. His two kinds are characterized by the 'steno-symbol' and the 'tensive-symbol'. 'Steno-symbols' are not only the words of science which have been reduced by choice, but also dead metaphors which custom has robbed of effectiveness. Wheelwright's comments on 'tensive-symbols' are even closer to Richards:

The tensive symbol cannot be entirely stipulative, inasmuch as its essential tension draws life from a multiplicity of associations, subtly and for the most part subconsciously interrelated, with which the symbol, or something like it and suggested by it, has been joined in the past, so that there is a stored up potential of semantic energy and significance which the symbol, when adroitly used, can tap. (page 94)

Richards would call these 'subtly interrelated multiplicities of associations', engrams. And his idea of their operation is very like Wheelwright's.

One more similarity may be noted before proceeding to the definition of metaphor suggested in *Metaphor and Reality*. Perhaps more than any of the critics previously considered Wheelwright insists on the essential role of metaphor and upon its ubiquity:

Thought is not possible to any significant degree without language, nor language without metaphoric activity whether open or concealed; the stabilization of certain metaphors into tensive symbols is a natural phase of the process . . . . When a straightforward thinker sets out to free himself from symbolic and metaphorical thinking, what he actually means to do is limit himself to those symbols and rigidified metaphors which have become habitual stereotypes in everyday life. The issue is not between symbolic and non-symbolic thinking, but between limiting one's thought and sensitivities to the plain meanings denoted by conventional symbols and learning to think with more tensive alertness. (page 128)

This too is familiar: "Plain speech is essentially inaccurate." But Hulme's terms are less mythic than are Wheelwright's: "Somehow in the long temporal mystery of evolution there emerged the power and disposition to let something – whether a body, an image, a sound, or later a written word – stand as surrogate for something else. Therein man became – and neither anthropologist nor philosopher can say when or how – a linguistic animal" (Intro., page 19).

Wheelwright's essential conception of metaphor is very like that of the New Critics: a metaphor is a 'war-embrace'. And the basic quality of that embrace is tension. Richards' terms, tenor and vehicle, are employed by Wheelwright in a way which must seem very strange to Richards, but the direction is the same:

Another kind of tension – one could say another dimension of it – arises from the overtones of universality that may be implied in an utterance. Such tension is typically found in the relationship, perhaps uncertain and wavering, between the situation as described or the succession of images as presented, and the stray glimpse of truth that they suggest without actually stating. It is in this sort of relationship that I. A. Richards' pair of words, *vehicle* and *tenor*, is most appropriately used: the one for the imagery or concrete situation described, the other for the ulterior significance that this suggests to the responsive imagination. (page 55)

The terms are here made metaphysical, rather than literary, and such a division as Wheelwright envisions, however real it may be, is of little value in the analysis of metaphor; rather, it demands an impressionism which must very rapidly become wholly personal. In his insistence on the function of poetry as a revealer of truth, Wheelwright is closer to Brooks than to Richards.

However, like Richards, Wheelwright considers metaphor to be the "element of tensive language that will serve best to reveal something of its nature" (page 70). First, Wheelwright insists that the grammatical distinction between metaphor and simile is worthless. He finds, rather, that "the test of essential metaphor is not any rule of grammatical form, but rather the quality of semantic transformation that is brought about" (page 71). Of course it is, but as I have argued in Chapter One, pages 30-31, above, the usual grammatical signal for metaphor is the absence of an explicit comparison. However, nothing prevents a poet from ignoring such a grammatical signal and yet producing metaphor.

Wheelwright is very much aware of the two sorts of poetic unity which I have called cognitive and experiential. In a manner reminiscent of Tate's manipulation of 'extension' and 'intension', Wheelwright examines the root of the word metaphor:

The transmutative process that is involved may be described as *semantic motion*; the idea of which is implicit in the very word "metaphor," since the motion (*phora*) that the word connotes is a semantic motion – the double imaginative act of outreaching and combining that essentially marks the metaphoric process. The outreaching and combining . . . are always combined to various degrees, at least implicitly. But as a means of understanding their respective contributions they may be examined singly, and may be called by distinguishing names – "epiphor" and "diaphor" – the one standing for the outreach and extension of meaning through comparison, the other for the creation of new meaning by juxtaposition and synthesis. (pages 71-72)

Epiphoric metaphor characteristically begins with a familiar object and its 'movement' (*phora*) is from that familiar object 'over on to' (*epi*) the less familiar term of the comparison. Wheelwright suggests that 'God the Father' is such an epiphor. An epiphor is metaphor in the 'conventional Aristotelian sense'. Its purpose is "to express a similarity between something relatively well known or concretely known . . . and something which, although of greater worth or importance, is less known or more obscurely known. Thus for an epiphor to operate there must be a discernable, literal ground between the known and the unknown" (pages 72-73). This sounds like a definition for 'analogy', but Wheelwright makes a distinction. If the comparison is too obvious, the tensive quality disappears, for "a tensive vibrancy can be achieved only where an adroit choice of dissimilars is made, so that the comparison comes as a shock which is yet a shock of recognition" (page 74). In the terms which I have been developing, the result of an epiphor is a cognitive unity: despite the initial strangeness of the juxtaposition, it is possible to discover that there is a logical basis for the assertion of identity. Thus the unity can be projected upon the artifact.

Although Wheelwright is aware that an agile manipulator can almost always discover epiphoric qualities in any juxtaposition and so create a cognitive unity, he asserts the possibility of a different sort of metaphor:

The other and complementary kind of semantic movement that metaphor engages may be called diaphor. Here the "movement" (phora) is "through" (*dia*) certain particulars of experience (actual or imagined) in a fresh way, producing new meaning by juxtaposition alone. (page 78)

At first this would appear to be an assertion that metaphor gives one thing for two – that each metaphor is a new word, but he does not mean quite what Stanford and Wimsatt mean. He is rather referring to a metaphor in which the two halves remain separate. Such, of course, is very nearly a contradiction in terms. He takes his clearest example from a "forgotten little magazine of the thirties":

> My country 'tis of thee
> Sweet land of liberty
>   Higgledy-piggledy my black hen.

Ransom might well call this an example of 'heterogeneity': the effect of the verse is produced by presenting cognitively unrelated elements as though they bore a cognitive relationship. The reader then seeks to discover a category to which both belong. Here a probable category is 'childish nonsense'. The problem is that once the reader has either discovered or created a class to which both halves of the diaphor belong, it ceases to be diaphoric and becomes epiphoric. That is, once a cognitive relationship has been discovered in an apparently experiential grouping, the grouping becomes in some degree cognitive.

Some time ago in a popular magazine there appeared an article on tests for creativity. One sort of test item provides the reader with a group of three words, apparently unrelated. The reader is to discover a fourth word which links the other three. For example: "tiger", "news", and "plate". Certainly these must initially seem to be related only because they are all three brought to attention at once. But once the reader discovers the key, 'paper', a cognitive relationship appears. Thus a really clever reader will eventually destroy all diaphors: only epiphors remain. Wheelwright is aware of this difficulty in his system:

The purest diaphor is doubtless to be found in non-imitative music and in the most abstract painting; for wherever any imitative or mimetic factor is present, whether an imitation of nature or of previous art or a mimesis of some recognizable idea, there is an element of epiphor. (page 79)

Thus the perception of pure diaphor is limited to trivial examples; it is a matter of immediate "pictorial and musical interest; as soon as the contrast is viewed in a larger context an element of epiphor peers forth" (page 80). Obviously, diaphor is not one-half of the poetic machine. Within Wheelwright's system it is only a valuable stage through which the reader progresses to cognitive unity. And for the reader who once solves the diaphor, it is available only through memory of the initial experience. Ransom might well accuse this system of the Eleatic Flaw, though it is clear that Wheelwright is seeking to avoid that very thing. For example, he finds Pound's "In a Station of the Metro" to be primarily diaphoric:

> The apparition of these faces in the crowd;
> Petals on a wet, black bough.

It is diaphoric because the similarity of the two images is "not so much antecedent as . . . induced . . . the association of ideas is based not on similarity but on emotional congruity" (page 80). Here, he suggests a division between emotion and cognition which is straight out of Richards. But Wheelwright admits that "it could be argued that the juxtaposition is tinged, faintly and subtly, with a degree of comparison". The problem is that for an Empsonian reader all things are related cognitively. Feeling and thought are not separate.

Wheelwright's conclusion as to the relationship between epiphor and diaphor is a sensible compromise. We need "to see the two processes . . . as intimately related aspects of poetic language and as mutually contributing to the power and significance of all good metaphor" (page 81). He seems to say that diaphor is largely a matter of the poet leaving out the connecting link between two images. He may do so intentionally, or he may have produced a comparison which is not a comparison. In any case, the reader must establish some relationship between the two images – whether that relationship consist of tone, attitude, or be produced by altering his original response to one of the pair in order to achieve congruity. (Of this the "My country / my black hen" is a perfect example.) The net effect of diaphor is to increase the possibility of plurisignification[7] by forcing the reader to create a relationship or a number of relationships, more or less cognitive, without finally insisting on a particular version. Wheelwright suggests that the greatest metaphors are those which do not separate epiphor and diaphor –

[7] The term plurisignification was apparently coined by Josephine Miles in a letter to *Kenyon Review*, II (1940), p. 502.

those in which "the two operate indissolubly as blended complementaries":

> My salad days,
> When I was green in judgment.

Cleopatra's defense certainly constitutes a master metaphor, but Wheelwright's epiphor/diaphor system does not account for its continued effectiveness. Once the grounds for the shift are discovered, the alien quality should disappear. Clearly problems remain, but in Wheelwright's development of Ransom's idea of heterogeneity there exists the first and largest of the many divisions which must be made if we are to understand the kinds of stimuli which produce the variety of reactions which the New Critics have to the motor of poetry—metaphor.

C. THE SYNCRETISM OF MURRAY KRIEGER

If, as W. K. Wimsatt suggests, our criticism should seek not a new course, but a combination of old ways, the The New Apologists for Poetry[8] moves in exactly the right direction:

> What I wish to do is to examine several theories – each inadequate and most of them inconsistent – in light of each other; to view them in terms of the problems of aesthetics; and to use them, so viewed, in order to point to those crucial questions on the answers to which a systematic apology depends. (page 7)

It may be well to set forth, briefly, the several theories which Krieger wishes to combine. They are familiar ones: first, he insists on the unity of the aesthetic object. Like Brooks, he denies the separateness of form and content, and, again like Brooks, he notes the heresy of paraphrase – and yet uses paraphrase as the first step in setting forth theory (page 26). But unlike Brooks he faces squarely the limitations of organicism: "How utterly self-contained can a poem be before its closed system would prove invulnerable to the reader's attempt to invade it . . . ? But of course the reader does find a way in, and this clearly indicates that his terms cannot be so utterly unuseable with respect to the contextually controlled terms within the poem" (page 21). This recognition that a poem is not in all its parts unique leads Krieger to insist upon a paradox:

[8] Murray Krieger, The New Apologists for Poetry (Minneapolis, 1956). Future references will be included in the text.

The poem must, in one sense, as a special form of discourse, be nonreferential, even as it must be referential to be any form of discourse at all. It must, as organic, be autonomous, even as it illuminates human experience. If it is to be the ground of the integrated, disinterested, even selfless experience I would denominate as aesthetic, the poem must be distinguished by what have been termed "immanent meanings," even though these cannot be discovered if I do not bring to the poem clearly specified meanings from the outside. (page 22)

Here Krieger delineates the problem which Hulme sought to escape with the notion of intensive manifolds perceived by intuition, and the problem which Wimsatt evades with the paradox of 'verbal icon'.

The second theory which Krieger wishes to incorporate is a theory of poetic composition parallel to Hulme's notion of the architect's steel curves held in place by the poet, and parallel to the structure-texture theory of Ransom. Language, it appears, has a certain will of its own:

I must say that the poet's original idea for his work, no matter how clearly thought out and complete he thinks it is, undergoes such radical transformations as language goes creatively to work upon it that the finished poem in its full internal relations, is far removed from what the author thought he had when he began. (page 23)

This is very like Richards' idea of the mutual interinanimation of words. Like Ransom, Krieger insists on the mutual modification of structure and texture, but he realizes that a chicken/egg paradox is involved: "In one sense the poet must be the creator of his work, directing its growth with his skills and in obedience to his intentions. Yet these intentions are continually modified and even transformed by the objective demands of an evolving context which seems to be creating its own intentions" (page 24). This is quite like Richards' definition of a word as the missing parts of its context. Krieger, as well as Ransom and Richards, runs the danger of intentional fallacy, but he realizes that the limitations suggested by Wimsatt apply.

The third theory upon which Krieger draws is the affective one:

Whatever theoretical claims I shall make must be construed as purely hypothetical, as the clause in the sentence which follows an "if" clause: if our interest is to deal adequately with this sort of poetic experience, then, in terms of this interest, what kind of object can we postulate which can facilitate this experience? What kind of creative process would be required to yield this kind of object? In what ways, besides affording us our experience of it, can we expect this kind of object to function for us? (page 19)

This assumes that the poetic experience is affective, and then suggests an examination of the stimulus in light of the response. Krieger differs from Richards in much the same way that Brooks and Wimsatt do: Krieger prefers the artifactual to the affective fallacy – though he is more aware of it than either Brooks or Wimsatt. He realizes that he is an affectivist making do with objective terms, though, like each of the critics considered above, on occasion he forgets that his statements are metaphorical.

One further observation concerning Krieger's heritage may be made before proceeding to his 'answers' to the aesthetic problems which he isolates. In the "Introduction" he gives a reading of Donne's "The Canonization" which suggests very strongly a debt to William Empson. Within the terms of this study, Krieger's syncretism is nearly complete. His theories are very like those of Richards, Ransom, and Brooks. He modifies the earlier theories in the ways suggested by Wimsatt, and he bases his critical comments upon a reading accomplished by the methods of Empson. Such a combination is vastly unsatisfactory if one is seeking a 'perfect' critical method which will allow a formula of poetic excellence. But given the elusive quality of poetry and the limitations of human intellect, the results which such a method produces are admirable. The temptation of the critic, says Krieger, is "to convert paradox into miracle" (page 27). It is perhaps true, as John Ciardi asserts, that "The minimum requirement for a good poem is a miracle." [9] Nevertheless, it is also true that the poet has a function quite different from that of the critic: the critic must work through paradox "without ignoring it or simply collapsing it" (page 27). These are brave words, and Krieger acknowledges that he means "to raise questions rather than to settle them". But the three major questions which he raises are just those which must be faced if a coherent theory of metaphor is to emerge from the welter of theory, speculation, interpretation, and polemic which makes up the New Criticism.

The three sections of The New Apologists for Poetry deal with "The Creative Process", "The Aesthetic Object", and "The Function of Poetry". And though Krieger does not mean just affectivism by 'function', nor just intention by 'creative', the distinctions which he makes are roughly those suggested by Wimsatt's work: intentional, artifactual, and affective. The principal difference is that Krieger extends each of the three to include materials and ideas which would seem to fall more naturally within the realms of philosophy, ontology, and epistemology, than of literary criticism. Since the creative effort of the poet is avail-

[9]   The Poetry Public Letter, II (1954), p. 13.

able only in its result, the poem, and since the poem is perceivable only through the process of reading, it would seem that a critic is in least danger of speaking nonsense when he concentrates his attention upon the poem as stimulus and seeks to determine the nature of that stimulus by examining the quality and quantity of response which he has to a poem.

It might seem that Richards' combination of impulses and Eliot's objective correlative accomplish this, but Krieger rejects both because, he says, they imply a complete poetic experience prior to the writing of the poem. He prefers an explanation parallel to Ransom's description of the creative struggle between structure and texture. "The idea becomes fresh as it is worked by him [the poet] across the grain of language habits. . . . Thus the idea does not merely take place in language; the language *is* the idea – an objectified and communicable phenomenon, not merely a mental and purely private one" (page 67). Krieger perceives that Ransom's work in *The New Criticism* is in many ways the most satisfactory statement of the poetic process, but in failing to understand that Ransom's central terms, structure and texture, are functional rather than ontological he accuses Ransom of a 'too persistent dichotomy' which prevents a 'true organicism'. Krieger does not mention Ransom's idea of heterogeneity and so does not note the possibility of two different sorts of unity – but of course to suggest two kinds of poetic unity is something of a contradiction in terms. Perhaps the reason Krieger is unable to discover or invent a satisfactorily organic theory of poetry is that totally organic poetry does not exist. Krieger has proved that we would be unable to recognize it if we met it.

Such an attitude comes near to denying the possibility of any sort of criticism beyond the historical or impressionistic. Krieger finds a means of circumventing such a conclusion which is parallel to the stimulus-response division which has been suggested for Richards. From Richards comes the notion of an affective unity which is organic. The unity is asserted to be not in the artifact, but in the reaction to the artifact. This prevents the reader from being excluded by artifactual organicism. The artifact can be considered, not as possessing an aesthetic unity, but as containing material which lends itself readily to the production of an experiential aesthetic unity in the reader. It is thus the function of criticism to examine the elements and proportions within the stimulus in the light of the particular sort of responsive unity which the critic experiences in reading the poem. Such a system avoids both the excesses of affective impressionism and the *cul-de-sac* of organic artifactualism; it is well on the way to positing the existence of cultural objects.

Krieger's rejection of this solution is based upon the contention that the poem as objective correlative must be only 'a shadowy middleman' (page 123). Such an assumption must be very short-sighted. It is like saying that if music is merely vibrations until an ear turns it into sound then there is nothing to be gained from analysing the nature of those vibrations. The difficulty which such an attitude leads him into is especially clear in his attack on Richards for saying that in some circumstances "'a carpet or a pot ... or a gesture'" may sometimes produce the same kind of reaction as does a poem. Such a statement, if true, makes "any attempt at criticism, organic or otherwise, seem pointless" (page 123). As we shall see shortly, Krieger is forced to admit Richards' assertion, though with different terminology.

In order to preserve the function of criticism, according to Krieger, Brooks "was forced to tear [irony] from the physiological context given it by Richards" (page 126). Brooks is given credit for accomplishing a correction achieved by Richards himself several years before the publication of *Modern Poetry and the Tradition*.[10] Richards' version seems much more satisfactory than does Brooks' in that it allows the critic to concentrate on the poem as artifact without forcing him to eliminate the function of the reader's world – which must not be left behind if he is to pronounce the words of the poem, much less understand them. Krieger, despite his praise of those who 'transformed' Richards, is forced to admit that problems are involved in the alteration:

I must concede, they do not betray any awareness that to get systematically at a theoretical account of the aesthetic object they should come by way of the reader's aesthetic experience as well as by way of the poet's creative act. (page 129)

Such a concession leads him back to a position which is much closer to that of Richards than to that of the transformers:

The [aesthetic] state will occur when it will occur, and to deny, for example, the power of nature to produce it would be to fly in the face of overwhelming testimony. But this definition of the aesthetic state does require that the object, natural or man-made, exercise some control over him and over the tendency in him to escape to his worldly interests. If it is a natural object to which he responds aesthetically, then either it has been given a form which can so control him, or he, thanks perhaps to the habits acquired in his commerce with art, projects such a form upon it and becomes an artist himself. (page 130)

[10]   This is the correction which Wimsatt, *Verbal Icon*, page 271, notes in Richards.

The argument has come full circle, but Krieger cannot rest here. If the object can in any way control the aesthetic experience, then it is the viewer's fault if he does not have the proper reaction; if the viewer projects the control into the object, "then this response is one that is idiosyncratic and that we cannot expect to be repeated" (page 130). The problems inherent in such a position are pretty obvious: the fact is that aesthetic states resulting from a view of 'natural' objects are as repeatable as any other kind. The reasons for this would seem to lie in the similarity of human beings and of their past experiences. The exploration of such reasons would lead to a study of myth and archetype which is beyond the present scope, but something of their mode is implied in the discussion of 'cultural norms' in Chapter Five, B, below.

Finally, Krieger solves the problem of artifactual-affective criticism by suggesting a new definition of 'objectivist'. "The objectivist would differentiate his position from that of the so-called absolutist with whom, unfortunately, he has invariably been identified" (page 159). Such a division is parallel to that suggested in *Coleridge on Imagination* between stimulus and response: there is to be a division between the aesthetic value of an object and the value of the aesthetic response to that object. Just how one is to arrive at the first without danger of corrupting it with the second, Krieger does not explain. What he wishes to gain by this division is clear and desirable:

Objectivism alone can, with logical consistency, at least give its proponent the knowledge that he may be wrong with respect to other judgments and not merely different from them: he is enabled to debate the issue. It can free him from the feeling of incorrigibility and, consequently, from the spiritual pride which underlies absolutism as well as relativism, and can return him to the humility which is both proper and profitable for an imperfect humanity striving to appreciate its noblest accomplishments. (page 163)

The distinction is between 'anchored' and 'unanchored' aesthetic value. "While he does not dispute the validity of subjective 'unanchored' values, he insists that these, belonging to the subjective experience rather than to the object, can, in view of his discussion of the aesthetic experience, claim no share in our critical judgment of the object as aesthetic" (page 161). Krieger has effected a transformation in the New Criticism, but it is a transformation back towards Richards. For the practical critic there would seem to be little difference between a division which names its halves 'anchored' and 'unanchored' and a division which is made up of elements attributable to the stimulus and elements attributable to the condition of the responding organism which were present prior to the experience. If there is a practical difference, it is that the second formulation suggests that the role of the reader is very important – that there may be an organicism in aesthetic perception as well as in aesthetic creation. The result of such a division is that in reading the work of William Empson (or for that matter Krieger's own rendering of "The Canonization") one may feel that the talented, sensitive reader is operating in a manner different from, but not inferior to, the initial creative act.

The practice, if not the theory, of the New Critics, their readings, indicates a clear recognition of the function of the reader. A reader must, in some degree, operate like the poet. The danger inherent in this attitude is that the reader will lose sight of the initial creative act in the admiration of his own. In a book designed as a companion for *The New Apologists for Poetry*, Richard Foster discovers instances of such impressionistic creation in the work of the New Critics. His major objection is that:

The very passion of its [the new criticism's] defense has bred chimeric images and visions, even diabolical arguments, a seductive rhetoric and poetry of critical discourse, in short, that would seem to lure us in hellish direction–toward the virtual heresies, born of romantic enthusiasms, of a religion of poetry.[11]

Such is hardly the case with the New Critics we have discussed. Foster makes his case by choosing a great plurality of his examples from the works of R. P. Blackmur, whose use of rhetoric is hardly typical of the New Criticism. Of course the critic must in some degree be impressionist as he attempts to catch the elusive golden fish which swim almost effortlessly through the net of his systems. If there existed a danger that the New Critics could be considered scientists: that they might think of themselves as dealing with literature under the circumstances of controlled experiments and so producing hypotheses and 'laws' which would enable man to predict and control the aesthetic universe in the way he now does the physical universe; then, Foster's book might be a necessary corrective lest the 'laws' be vitiated by the inclusion of the human element. The danger does not seem very real. Foster does, however, sum up an attitude which appears over and over again in the works of the New Critics:

I. A. Richards, who has really done so little as a practical critic (and very little more, though he has *written* a lot, as a "theorist"), has almost single-

---

[11] Foster, *The New Romantics*, p. 189.

handedly motivated the modern critical revolution by haranguing against modern man's educated inabilities to read and understand. And, again almost singlehandedly, he has institutionalized the key concepts of the revolution – "Imagination," the complexity of language's "meaning" as experience, and the bogey of "stock response," which fathered psychologistically the New Critics' descriptions of good poetry in terms of "irony," "paradox," "tension," "impurity"–largely through the pure fervor of his wonder at the ways of words. (page 198)

The tone of faint praise seems out of place when juxtaposed with the list of accomplishments which Foster grants Richards.

Krieger's value for the present study is that he formulates in clear terms the aesthetic problems which must be faced before a critic has the right to set up shop. His answers to the questions he raises are generally consistent with the implications of the critics discussed in previous chapters. And though he does not greatly advance their theories, his formularizations achieve a synthesis without which the place they occupy in the history of criticism is difficult to discern.

IV

THEORY AND APPLICATION

> – A wise beginning for any large inquiry is to entertain
> the postulate that reality, or a goodly part of it, is not
> obvious and discoverable by overt public methods of
> investigation, but is latent, subtle, and shy .... If we
> cannot hope ever to be perfectly right, we can perhaps
> find both enlightenment and refreshment by changing,
> from time to time, our ways of being wrong.
>
> *Metaphor and Reality*

A. A GRAMMAR OF METAPHOR

The most extreme problem which the practical critic must face is the
necessity to decide to what degree his 'manifestation' of the poem is an
accurate representation of cultural norms: to sort out elements of
response which result from his individual, as opposed to cultural,
experience: to decide what the 'cultural norm' in a particular case is.
If the 'norm' is thought of as an 'ideal', then, in familiar Platonic
fashion, the poem is said to have an existence outside any individual,
its documentation becomes an imitation of an imitation, and the response to the poem by a reader becomes a third remove from the
poem's 'essence'. If, on the other hand, norm is taken to mean average,
then an appeal to a common denominator of meaning would seem to
be the way to separate the 'cultural' from the 'individual' reading. But
of course we know that the 'best' response to a poem is perhaps as far
removed from the 'average' as is the worst. In such case, the problem
is turned around: the critic must decide which deviations from the norm
represent improvements upon and which represent reductions of the
average meaning of the poem. Such an approach would involve statis-
tical compilations of various readings, the development of skewed or
bell-shaped curves and so forth. Because of the intensive nature of
verbal art AND its manifestations, such an approach is futile.

As we have seen, the New Critics managed this problem by setting up touchstones, poems and passages of which they approved, and then tried to isolate the particular qualities which such passages shared. They chose such terms as 'tension', 'irony', 'impurity', 'inclusiveness', and 'unified sensibility' to indicate the quality which informs poetry of 'the first rank'. Such a decision inevitably chooses 'metaphysical' poetry as supreme and labels 'neo-classical' poetry inferior. Manifestly, this will not do. At best, the New Critical theory treated a section of cultural norms as the whole, and at worst it established idiosyncratic response as cultural norm.

A second major problem of practical criticism is that delineated by Hulme. If the poem is an intensive manifold, all attempts to separate its vectors move away from, rather than toward, an awareness of the totality of poetic experience. Since analytical criticism, by definition, treats parts separately, the only logical functions of criticism would seem to be historical and impressionistic. There is, however, a false premise involved, based upon mistaking the vehicle of a metaphor for its tenor. A poem is said to be 'organic', to be 'living'. The metaphor is a biological one, and tends to invalidate all practical criticism, most notably paraphrase. Since we know that a 'living thing', once taken apart, loses its life and if put back together will no longer be alive, it would seem to follow that a poem-as-biological-entity is subject to the same rule. Clearly such is not the case. A poem has no 'quintessence', no 'miracle of life' which escapes irretrievably when the poem is 'dismembered'. If we must have a metaphor on this level, it might be better to use machine. The critic as mechanic can assemble and disassemble a poem endlessly without damage to the poem as functioning unit. The only 'life' a poem has is its ability to call forth particular organizations of cultural elements, and examining the norms of culture is much more like analysing a machine than dissecting an animal. The holism implicit in the biological metaphor results in viewing the critic as vivisectionist, even when it allows such experiments in the 'interest of science'.

The dangers of the mechanical metaphor are clear. If a poem is made up of definable parts, is it not possible to find a blueprint for poetry? To devise a formula that will allow poems to be produced on demand? While it might be argued that a great deal of 'poetry' is so produced and that schools of poets are identifiable precisely because they make some use of such blueprints, such is not the question at hand. The function of criticism is descriptive, not prescriptive, and the critic must not mistake his analysis for the poem, any more than he must mistake criticism for literature.

If the limitations involved in Empson's biological metaphor are recognized his statement of practical method is reasonable, though it by no means settles the problems which have just been raised. A critic must react to a poem sensitively and definitely:

and then, having fixed the reaction ... must be able to turn the microscope on it with a certain indifference and without smudging it with [his] fingers ... and have enough detachment not to mind what [his] sources of satisfaction may turn out to be. (*Seven Types*, page 279.)

If we read the 'it' of Empson's definition as 'manifestation of verbal art', we have a possible approach to the two major problems in practical criticism. (1) It is the critic's own manifestation upon which he operates. (2) That manifestation is revised and corrected in the process of analysis so as to reduce the incidence of purely idiosyncratic elements in his manifestation. It is undesirable that all the purely 'personal' elements be eliminated. For whatever 'life' a poem has is maintained in part by the interaction between the reader as individual and the norms upon which the poem draws. Just as verbal art is refreshed by the dynamic nature of cultural norms and language codes, so too the perception of poetry is constantly renewed by the ultimately ineradicable individualism of every reader.

It is now possible to set forth the system of metaphorical analysis suggested (and employed) by our New Critics. Their major accomplishment lies in treating the individual manifestation as extensive while yet recognizing its intensive nature. Since the manifestation does not 'die' when it is taken apart, and since it can be put back together with a greater 'interinanimation' than it may have originally possessed, there is no danger to the poem or to the reader in such a method, unless, of course, the reader mistakes analysis for poetry. The 'Grammar of Metaphor' which I here present falls far short of the complexity of Richards' systems, but it therefore runs less risk of becoming an end in itself. Its comparative simplicity allows for the variations in reading which are caused by the unique psychological context of the individual reader and at the same time encourages the reader to judge his own reactions against those which constitute cultural norms.

The first of the divisions to be made between classes of juxtaposed images is that suggested by Ransom and Wheelwright. When two engrams, manifest in response to two artifactual stimuli, are present in a mind at the same time, they either combine or remain separate. It is clear that any such juxtaposition has at least experiential unity in that a single mind perceives both elements, but such basic unity differs radically from both emotional and rational unity. Emotional unity is achieved when both elements fit within a single emotional context, when the reader reacts similarly to both. Rational unity is the result of perceiving more or less empirically verifiable similarities in the two elements. In both emotional and rational unity the perceiver feels that there resides in the stimuli (more properly in the engrams which are called up) a basic similarity, even if the similarity is only the ability to elicit parallel emotional responses in the reader.

The effect of purely experiential unity is very different. To produce emotional or rational unity, the mind searches for similarities and rests, at least temporarily, in the satisfaction of perceiving a pattern which is comprehensible to the mind and which at the same time is based upon a pattern in that which is perceived. In pure experiential unity the mind is baffled in its attempts to discover (or project) comprehensible similarities in the engrams. The stasis which the mind is forced into is that of acceptance or rejection, an acknowledgment of a heterogeneity which resists the connecting function of the mind. At its best, unity gives the reader a sense of power, coupled with a wonder at the ability of the mind to perceive and impose patterns. Simultaneity, at its best, humbles the reader with a sense of his own limited power. Rather than becoming an observer who measures and weighs, he is drawn into the vast heterogeneity of experience and forced to recognize that the pattern of experience is not a human creation nor is it completely susceptible to reason. A true paradox achieves such heterogeneity.[1]

Of course all unity includes simultaneity, and it is within the power of the synthesizing imagination to create some degree of unity within almost any juxtaposition. It is a nice discrimination to discover the separate effects of the two; both are included in the experience of a

---

[1]   Erich Fromm, D. T. Suzuki, and Richard De Martino, *Zen Buddhism and Psychoanalysis* (New York, 1960). Suzuki's essay opens with a comparison of a Bashō haiku with Tennyson's "Flower in the Crannied Wall". Dr. Suzuki makes exactly the same point. Although a complete investigation of 'juxtaposition' would have to treat simultaneity in depth, the particular nature of this study forces a concentration on degrees of unity. I do not imply that the juxtapositions pointed to by Dr. Suzuki are unimportant, but that for New Criticism and metaphysical poetry they are not the point at issue. The relationships between negative metaphor and pure simultaneity are not so close as they at first may appear. In fact, positive metaphor is in many ways closer to simultaneity in its effect on the reader. Ultimately both positive and negative metaphor depend upon degrees of cognition, upon plucking the flower from the crannied wall; hence, they are radically different from the sort of acceptance posited by Dr. Suzuki.

poem. To treat them separately is to falsify the total poetic experience. But such is the problem in any system of analysis. To get the experience, and to get it whole, the reader must read the poem, not an analysis of its metaphors. In the actual reading of a poem there cannot even be a clear-cut distinction between the affective and artifactual: a distinction which my previous chapters have insisted upon at some length. In borderline cases judgments of the nature of the cultural object must appeal either to the individual reader or to some sort of common denominator because the cultural object can be examined only as it is manifest. Of the two, I prefer the former; the common denominator must limit very sharply the richness of poetic communication. The individual experience is a much fuller communication which, it must be granted, in extreme cases may not be 'communication' at all.

Ultimately, the division between unity and simultaneity must be made by each reader, and the 'division' is not a conscious one. It can be got at only by working back from the affective response. Since such a response can be examined only introspectively, it is clear that criticism is unlikely to be replaced by one or more 'ologies' which seek the exactness of predictability. However, once these limitations are realized, a good deal may be gained by speaking AS IF the discriminations and categories which can be devised have greater objective validity than they actually do. Such is Krieger's position: everything one may say about art must be considered to follow an 'if' clause. The implicit 'if' may be recognized by softening the assertive tone when a response seems to extend far beyond the limits of the common denominator of meaning related to a word.[2]

The difference between heterogeneity and unity can be perceived clearly in the case of puns. The crudest effect of a pun is achieved by focusing the reader's attention upon one meaning of a word and then, by manipulating syntax, suddenly switching his attention to another meaning. Whether the pun operates by juxtaposing two meanings of the same word, or by juxtaposing two words which sound alike, or by shifting two words which are pronounced differently to an intermediate pronunciation, the effect is achieved by the surprise which results when the reader perceives that a meaning quite different from that which he expected is present. If the two meanings cannot be applied to a single context, the result is heterogeneity. Such puns occur frequently in humor: the familiar shaggy-dog stories which conclude with "Brother,

---

[2]   For a discussion of tied and free imagery see Richards, *Principles of Literary Criticism*, pp. 116 ff.

can you SPEAR a dime?" or in more complex fashion with "Transporting young gulls across the state lion for immortal porpoises" are cases in point. Quibbles often depend on a similar process. Question: "Mister, have you got thirty cents for a sandwich?" Answer: "Let me see the sandwich first." Poets are more subtle, but the principle is much the same. In such cases the two meanings are not made relevant to the same rational context. The effect is of heterogeneity, but the reader is, in the case of jokes, amused rather than humbled. On a much higher level, many haiku operate by means of such juxtapositions, though the effect is quite different since the reader seeks unity between the disparates, and failing to find it, is encouraged to accept rather than control.[3]

However, a pun may achieve unity. When Donne begs that God's 'sunne' continue to shine, the notion of corresponding planes allows the reader to see that both tenor and vehicle are included in what at first appears to be a single word: such a pun is a metaphor. There is ground for metaphorical shift, and the two meanings are read as if they were equated rather than simply juxtaposed. The most basic difference between the usual metaphor and the usual pun is that whereas a pun yields two things from one, a metaphor gives one thing for two. The pun, however, gives up the single meaning, or rather maintains two single meanings side by side. The metaphor maintains the individual meanings of both 'words' at the same time that it combines them to form a new meaning. This new meaning is metaphor. In its equation of disparate meanings, metaphor achieves a juxtaposition which is transformed into a superimposition of the one term upon the other. The effect is of neither the one nor the other, nor yet the simple combination of the two, but of a third meaning which can be expressed in no other way. In a sense, each metaphor is a new word, a word which encourages the exploration of free meanings without giving up the tied meanings of its constituent parts. The tied meaning of a metaphor is very difficult to determine; hence, the existence of metaphor is a primary reason for the inadequacy of paraphrase. A pun-metaphor is often very effective because it requires two stages of perception. First the reader must discover the two meanings suggested by a single word, and then he must see that the two meanings may be combined to produce a third meaning – first two things for one, then one thing for two.

[3] There are various degrees of heterogeneity in haiku, and there are haiku which depend upon cognitive unity. But most often the goal seems to be to give man an awareness, rather than an understanding, of his situation.

Pun-metaphors, like 'sunne', present only the vehicle; the reader must discover for himself (with the aid of context) the tenor. Such a metaphor may be called 'submerged'.[4] The more usual metaphor presents both tenor and vehicle. Consider an instance from George Herbert:

> Wit's an unruly engine
> (*The Church Porch*, stanza 30).

Here we have a basic metaphor: one thing is said to be another; the predication is simple and clear. Were the two juxtaposed rather than equated, there might appear to be little similarity between 'wit' and 'engine', but granted the predication, it takes but a moment's attention to perceive that the two can be considered within the same framework of meaning. One is superimposed upon the other, and a creative flurry of aesthetic perception occurs. The primary category of meaning which contains both 'wit' and 'engine' is 'agency' or 'tool'; from this initial ground for metaphorical shift it is possible to discover many others: 'complexity', 'mechanical nature', 'a tendency to break down', and so forth. The adjective 'unruly' serves at the same time to suggest and to limit the grounds which will be applicable. For example, 'made of iron' will not do. Such basic metaphors, in which both tenor and vehicle are named at approximately the same time may be called 'surface metaphors' as distinguished from 'submerged metaphors'.

If the combination of engrams which results from metaphor is equated with the engram called forth by a succeeding word, the process of combination is repeated. The grounds for the first metaphorical shift tend to extend to the new combination, and grounds which were rejected in the perception of the first metaphor tend to be rejected in the succeeding shift. This is to say that the grounds for an initial metaphor set a pattern of association – create an expectancy in the mind of the reader – which must be fulfilled or violated. Aspects of succeeding combinations which support that pattern are accepted more readily than are those grounds which move in directions contrary to the pattern. Donne's "She is all states, and all princes I" is a clear example of the fulfillment of such an expectation. The particular grounds for combining 'princes' and 'I' are determined in large part by the grounds for combining 'she' and 'states'. The most obvious ground for this particular shift is microcosm. But of course the violation of expectation is one of the basic ways in which a poet can produce tensive language. Shakespeare's "Sonnet 130" ("My mistress' eyes") achieves its effect

---

[4] Submerged metaphor is examined in greater detail later in this chapter.

by such violation. The horde of Petrarchan conceits which claim deity
for mistresses provides the expectation which Shakespeare violates at
length.

Theoretically, the associative pattern (followed or violated or alter-
nately followed and violated) could continue indefinitely. Metaphors
could be made complex by incorporating additional meanings or compound by combining with succeeding metaphors (as in She/States –
Princes/I). Practically, the number of combinations is limited. Since
the linkings occur, not among the words themselves, but in the engrams
which the words evoke in the mind of the reader, the number of combinations is limited by the capacity and sophistication of the particular
reader's mind.[5] An especially strong pattern may allow for an extended
use of the same shift, or lack of shift.

So far, the concentration has been upon the similarities between
tenor and vehicle which enable the reader to perceive the unity of
metaphor, but there is an opposite force which operates, in varying
degrees, within each metaphor: the special identity of tenor which refuses to combine totally with vehicle, and the resistance of vehicle to a
complete subordination to tenor. To call metaphor 'duple unity' suggests that the third meaning which comes into existence with the equation of tenor and vehicle is achieved by balancing attractions and repulsions between the engrammatic complexities suggested in the reader's
mind by the two words. The proportions of attraction and repulsion
vary greatly from metaphor to metaphor. If a continuum is constructed
to represent this variation, we have at one extreme the 'positive' metaphor and at the other extreme the 'negative' metaphor.

A positive metaphor is one whose primary effect is achieved by
means of attractions (similarities) between the engrammatic tenor and
the engrammatic vehicle.[6] The 'perfect' positive metaphor would be
one in which the unity of tenor and vehicle is complete. The conception
of metaphor as duple unity denies the name metaphor to such complete
unification. Since there is felt to be no difference between the two
words, the original tenor disappears. It is possible to think of all sub-
stantives as being such 'dead' metaphors: hence the total metaphorical
nature of language. But there is a class of 'dead' metaphor which might

---

[5] Seymour Chatman, *A Theory of Meter* (The Hague, 1965), examines such
temporal determinants as they apply to rhythm, pp. 18-29.
[6] For convenience of diction, I speak as though tenor, vehicle, and metaphor
referred to the artifact. They refer to the various engrams and their combinations
which result from the stimuli of the artifact as a coded manifestation of cultural
object, rather than to the artifact itself.

better be regarded as 'moribund'. Such words as the 'arm' of a chair, the 'head' of an engine, or the 'horn' of a saddle can be revived by calling attention to the forgotten differences between the general and the specific uses of the word. Such metaphors differ from submerged metaphors in that their tenors are not concealed but rather forgotten. This distinction is engrammatic rather than artifactual. For someone who has never heard the moribund metaphor its effect is that of a submerged metaphor: he at once seeks the tenor for the vehicle 'arm', or 'head', or 'horn'. The determining factor is the mental context of the reader, the degree to which he shares the particular cultural norm. In general usage, however, a distinction between moribund and submerged may be established by reference to the customary effect of a word, but of course the 'effect' of words is dynamic.

If both tenor and vehicle are named, the 'positive' metaphor cannot be wholly unified. The reader is aware of the separate identities of both halves: identities which refuse to allow complete unity. The most positive of surface metaphors would be made up of an infinite number of similarities and a single disparity. Since the similarities are engrammatic rather than artifactual it is difficult if not impossible to establish the exact degree of positiveness of a metaphor taken out of context: a context made up of the artifactual context of the poem, the situational context of the poet, and the mental context of the reader – all three are partially, but not completely, determined by social norms. A skillful poet may force the reader to keep a number of possible degrees of positiveness in mind until the entire poem has been read.

At the opposite end of the continuum, the negative, are heterogeneous puns and juxtapositions which achieve only experiential unity. The 'perfect' negative metaphor would be one in which the disparity between tenor and vehicle is complete. Once again, duple unity denies the name of metaphor to such a juxtaposition. Since there is felt to be no unity, there can be no metaphor. But, like the discriminations among degrees of positive metaphor, the exact quality of a negative metaphor can be determined only in the light of the total context of the image, a context which must include the poet, the poem, the reader, and cultural norms. One has only to glance through the readings of Empson to realize the enormous resistance to such total disparity, and to perceive the inventiveness of which the mind is capable when faced with a suggested equation which is not an equation. To summarize: metaphor is duple unity. It must allow for the combination of tenor and vehicle so that they produce one thing for two, but it must not combine the two so successfully that they completely lose their separate identities. Metaphors exist only between the two ends of the positive-negative continuum: at either end they vanish.

It is possible to distinguish among metaphors according to the nature of their duple groupings. If neither tenor nor vehicle is itself a metaphor, the result is a 'simple' metaphor. If either half is itself a metaphor, the new metaphor is 'complex'. If both tenor and vehicle are themselves metaphors, the new metaphor is 'compound'. The value of these distinctions does not lie in assigning terms to particular metaphors, but in the increased awareness of the cultural object which results from the analysis. If the grammarian's sin is not avoided, the system is worse than useless.

So far, three principles of classification have been suggested: unity-heterogeneity; simple-compound-complex; and positive-negative. The first classification establishes what is and what is not a metaphor. The second is a formal classification; without its simplifying operation all but the most basic kind of metaphor resist analysis. The third classification is of greater significance, for it is the positive-negative polarity of a metaphor which for the new critics determines its particular function within a poem. The importance of this polarity will be illustrated in the readings which conclude this chapter.

A further classification may be examined before proceeding to analysis of specific metaphors. Just as there are metaphors which name both their halves – both tenor and vehicle – too there are metaphors which name only their vehicle, 'submerged' as opposed to 'surface' metaphors. It is also possible to submerge vehicles of compound metaphors. Donne's "Holy Sonnet XIV" opens with a useful example:

> Batter my heart, three personed God; for, you
> As yet but knocke, breathe, shine, and seeke to mend;
> That I may rise, and stand, o'erthrow mee, and bend
> Your force, to breake, blowe, burn and make me new.

The tenor 'heart' is synecdochical for 'self' and emblematic of soul, but both these metaphoric movements are moribund. If, for the sake of illustration, we also pass over the Biblical association of Christ knocking at the door, of God breathing life, and of Christianity as the light of the world, it is possible to see a submerged metaphor in operation. That metaphor may be found by answering a riddle. The tenor, 'heart', asks: "My vehicle is available as a term which unifies the following attributes: to the breathed upon, shined, and mended; to be broken, blown upon, fired, and made anew. What is my vehicle?" The 'answer' is 'metal vessel'. Hence the metaphor is heart-metal vessel. An intertwined metaphor of God as tinker or alchemist also emerges. Thus there are two submerged metaphors which unify the passage, advance its argument, and establish the firmness in logical (or pseudo-logical) progression which is a hallmark of Donne's poetry.

Consider another example, Shakespeare's "Sonnet 146":

> Poor soul, the centre of my sinful earth,
> Thrall to these rebel pow'rs that thee array,
> Why dost thou pine within and suffer dearth,
> Painting thy outward walls so costly gay?
> Why so large cost, having so short a lease,
> Dost thou upon thy fading mansion spend?
> Shall worms, inheritors of this excess,
> Eat up thy change? Is this thy body's end?

Although it is clear that Shakespeare intends no puzzle, the tenor, 'body', for the vehicle, 'earth', is not expressed until line eight, though it is suggested by the idea of microcosm, by mentioning 'sinful earth' as the antithesis of 'soul', and through various associative connections such as that between 'earth' and 'dust to dust'. Shakespeare gives alternative vehicles for body – 'rebel pow'rs', 'outward walls' – the tenor of which is suspended. 'Inheritors' suggests that 'excess' is vehicle for 'legacy' which is in turn vehicle for 'body'. The contrasting values of 'excess' and 'legacy' produce a negative quality in the doubly submerged metaphor which is very much in keeping with the tone of the poem. Here we can see a further distinction: since Shakespeare eventually gives the answer, 'body', his body-earth metaphor is suspended, rather than submerged.

A further, simpler, example may make this idea clearer. Consider the kenning 'whale-road': the tenor is 'sea', the vehicle 'road'. The poet names only the vehicle, and then chooses a traveler who uses the sea as man uses a road, 'whale'. Depending upon the artifactual context and upon the psychological context of the reader, 'whale-road' may be either positive or negative. If the effect is to make tame the wild by expressing it in familiar terms, if the whale and the man are felt to be akin, the result is positive. But if the distinctions between a man and a whale are emphasized, the effect is to make the unknown more terrible by contrasting it with the known. In such a case the resulting metaphor is negative. For 'whale-road' to be positive, it is necessary that the reader mute the obvious differences between man and whale. This may be done as a result of contextual signals in the poem or as a result of poetic convention or as a result of the familiarity of the image. In any case the submersion of the tenor, 'sea', encourages the reader to insist upon the relevance of his particular psychological context – a context which is to some degree unique even as it is strongly influenced by cultural norms.

Obviously, submerged and suspended metaphors allow the reader a greater share of creativity than do surface metaphors. In the kenning a broad clue to the tenor is given by 'whale'. In Shakespeare's sonnet the reader is provided with a number of hints and may finally check his conclusion against the answer which is given later in the poem. Such is not always the case. Donne's "Sonnet XIV" gives neither answer nor obvious clue. To choose a modern example, Wallace Stevens often asks the reader to discover both tenor and intent of the metaphor by creating subsidiary tenors which may or may not correspond to those discovered by other readers. His "Someone Puts a Pineapple Together" illustrates the manner in which various tenors may be created for existing vehicles. The poet sees a pineapple and lists twelve possible tenors while suggesting a dozen more. So too, the reader when confronted with an artifactual pineapple (which does not make clear the limitations of tenor) creates successive tenors in an effort to construct a ladder of analogy which will allow him to unify as many elements of the poem as possible. Ultimately, the metaphorical meaning which is conveyed by the combination of all possible tenors and vehicles is vast beyond paraphrases:

> It is that which is distilled
> In the prolific ellipses that we know,
>
> In the planes that tilt hard revelations on
> The eye, a geometric glitter, tiltings
> As of sections collecting toward the greenest cone.[7]

The particular virtue of submerged metaphor is that it, more easily than surface metaphor, insists that the poem BE an experience for the reader, rather than the PRESENTATION of an experience of the author. When it is skillfully used, the poet is able to communicate not only the result of aesthetic creation, but something of the process of creation itself. That the 'creation' accomplished by the reader may differ in important ways from the creation of the poet is both a danger and a virtue.

The systems of classification suggested above teach the essence of

---

[7] Wallace Stevens, *Poems by Wallace Stevens* (New York, 1957), p. 139.

metaphor no more than grammar teaches the essence of language. But like the study of grammar, an application of these classifications insists upon a close inspection of the total context of the poem, during the course of which a good deal may be learned about the ways of metaphor. It is in the close examination of specific images that the New Critics make their greatest contributions.

B. THREE METAPHORS

Now that four divisions have been suggested for the analysis and classification of metaphor, those divisions may be tested upon metaphors taken from metaphysical poetry in order to determine their usefulness – to discover if a simple, surface, positive metaphor is significantly different in function from a compound, submerged, negative metaphor, and to see if that difference can be attributed to the characteristics which identify the divisions. It is convenient to speak of the linkings and repulsions as if they were wholly external and as if they operated identically in every reading of the poem; the very nature of poetry dictates that they do not. The critic must deal with his own manifestation of the cultural object rather than with the object itself. He must then analyze as an extensive manifold the intensive manifold of his perception.

My method is to begin with a very common metaphor and move to metaphors of a more complicated nature. For the sake of brevity, the three metaphors discussed below are treated as though they were distinct from the larger poetic context in which they appear; they are to be regarded as further explication of the divisions established in section one of this chapter as well as test cases. For a treatment of metaphors as they interact with the larger context of the poem (intentional, artifactual, affective, and cultural), see the reading of Donne's "Epithalamion made at Lincolnes Inn" which makes up section three of this chapter. I assume that the manifestations of verbal art which I perceive are within the appropriate circle of cultural response; they may not always be so.

As an example of metaphor in its most basic form, consider two lines from Edward Herbert:

> Now that the April of your Youth adorns
> The Garden of your face . . . .[8]

[8]   Edward Herbert, "Dittie", *The Poems of Edward Herbert*, ed. by G. C. Moore Smith (Oxford, 1923).

Were it not for the long tradition of such images, 'garden-face' might be classified as heterogeneous rather than as unified, but the linking of the two has been spelled out so often that their similarities are at once available to anyone familiar with the traditions of Renaissance poetry: cherries–lips; fragrance–breath; bird song–voice; roses and lilies–cheeks; fountains–eyes; and so on to ingenuity's end. That these traditions are part of nearly every reader's equipment is attested by the junior high school wit which asserts: "Your lips are like petals, bicycle pedals." Were the poet to juxtapose 'ruined garden' and 'face', an equally bulky list of similarities is suggested by the inversion of the tradition. In either case there are enough engrammatic similarities to produce a metaphor. If the image which results is taken literally, 'cherries–lips' is only slightly less ridiculous than 'lips–pedals'. But metaphor is not simply the combination of tenor and vehicle taken separately. There must always be a selection of qualities, and a muting of other qualities. Otherwise, all images would be heterogeneous. In the case of 'garden–face' the mind moves so readily to a metaphor that the peculiarities of garden which do not apply to an attractive female face are muted. That discrepancies are available is made clear by the example of 'lips–pedals' as well as the tradition of 'ruined garden–face'. The poet, if he will, can manipulate syntax in such a manner as to insist on such details of 'garden–face' as size, inhabitants, shape, and the necessity for fertilizing and transplanting. Herbert does not do so.

If the tensive possibilities of 'garden–face' are so muted, why does the reader not feel it to be worthless as a poetic image? The answer is twofold. Not all of the tensions are muted. Since 'garden–face' is surface (both tenor and vehicle are named), the difference between the two is recognized, even though attention is directed to similarities rather than differences. The second reason is more complex. Hulme, Richards, and especially Brooks, condemn (at least in theory) all such metaphors. What once may have been a good ('tensive') metaphor has lost its power. The insistence of the New Critics that poetry must involve 'tension', or 'paradox', or 'ambiguity' dictates that such metaphors as 'garden–face' must either be revived by shifting the context in which they appear, or they must be discarded. Renewal in this case might be achieved by forcing upon the reader's attention such details as size and shape. Clearly, Lord Herbert does no such thing. The metaphor which precedes 'garden–face' is 'April–youth'. In its conjoining of seasonal 'April' with human 'youth', Herbert points away from tension rather than toward it. If 'April–youth' is to mean anything at all, attention must be given to attributes which are shared by young women and spring. April as the cruelest month must NOT be considered. Thus the pattern of metaphorical shift set by 'April–youth' intensifies the positive quality of the succeeding metaphor, 'Garden–face'. The account which the New Critics make of the source of such 'dead' metaphors as these two is sensible enough,[9] but it ignores the value of metaphors which count on the reader to 'mute' tensions, and such metaphors are not 'dead' in the sense which Hulme condemns.

The difference between 'moribund' and 'muted' metaphor is largely a matter of strategy. The imagery which Hulme rejects ('Arrow', 'heart', and 'the rest of it'[10]) seeks the reader's applause for discovering a similarity between such apparently opposite activities as war and love. It counts on tension for its effects. But once the similarity between tenor and vehicle has been granted – and in this case it has been granted for a very long time – such metaphors if they claim tensiveness can only offer stale wit. That to young or inexperienced readers such images may offer insight into the nature of the battle of the sexes only emphasizes the importance of the reader's context, of his possessing the cultural norms of his group. Just as a young reader may fail to mute and so misread a poem, so too he may mute too readily and so accomplish the poet's work. The infamous "Trees" is a case in point. It counts on the reader to mute dissimilarities which a sophisticated reader refuses to ignore. By equating such widely disparate items as artifact and vegetable ("A poem lovely as a tree"), Kilmer asks that the dissimilarities between future concretions be ignored. The beginner is willing to do so and accepts 'A nest of robins' in the tree's 'hair' with no difficulty. The experienced reader boggles. The image is made acceptable neither by tradition nor by the kind of pseudo-logical structure which enables a skillful reader to accept such conceits in the poetry of Donne. Kilmer elaborates the basic metaphor, 'poem–tree', into a conceit – a conceit in which he substitues 'woman' for poem, 'infant', for woman and so fails to maintain consistency in progression of vehicle. The experienced reader complains that the poet has not done his share.[11] Many of John Cleveland's poems present the same sort of difficulty.

While it may be true that the first poet to use 'garden–face' felt in it

[9] See *The New Criticism*, pp. 77-78.
[10] Hulme, *Speculations*, says "Nothing could be more dead now than the conventional expressions of love poetry, the arrow which pierces the heart and the rest of it" (p. 151).
[11] Cleanth Brooks and Robert Penn Warren, *Understanding Poetry*, 3rd ed. (New York, 1965), reach much the same conclusion, for similar reasons.

all the tensive force of 'Busy old fool, unruly sun', and that the in-experienced reader may yet mistake it for a metaphor of tension, it is, I think, clear that Herbert chose it BECAUSE it lacked tension. He asks the reader not to experience the shock of recognition, but to recognize with quiet pleasure the grace and vitality which nature evidences in spring flowers – human as well as vegetable. The delicate and momen-tary attention which he grants 'April–youth' and 'Garden–face' signals to the perceptive reader that the metaphors are to be read as positive rather than as negative. Though the stillness which such strategy evokes is duller than the strife of a negative metaphor, the reader may sometimes enjoy a pause from the violence of the war-embrace.

There are, then, two sorts of 'positive' metaphor: the kind in which a poet, striving for tension, unwisely chooses a tenor and vehicle which have too long been fellows – no quarrel remains between them. Such a positive metaphor is, to the experienced reader, simply trite. When 'arrows–eyes' is presented as a witty discovery, the reader can only regret the poet's poverty of imagination. But when a positive metaphor such as 'Garden–face' is presented as an old acquaintance whose famili-arity is claimed as a grace, the result is a quiet lyric. The pleasure which such a metaphor produces is that which Aristotle claims as the most basic attraction of art. It is the pleasure of simple recognition – the stock-in-trade of fairy stories, romances, and epics. So long as both poet and reader realize that positive metaphors operate differently, with different effects, from negative metaphors, all is well. If a poet mistakes a positive for a negative metaphor, the effect will be, for an experienced reader, pretentiously flat; an inexperienced reader, mistaking positive for negative, misjudges the poem.

A second example of metaphor, from George Herbert's "The Flower", operates quite differently from 'Garden–face':

> Who would have thought my shrivel'd heart
> Could have recover'd greenesse?[12]

Here the basic metaphor is 'heart–flower'. This is a surface metaphor because both tenor and vehicle are named, though 'flower' is partially submerged in that it is represented by two of its possible conditions. Since the tenor of the image suggested by 'shrivel'd' and 'greenesse' is named in the title of the poem, and since the two are metonymic rather than disparate, the submersion is slight. However the tenor of the

---

[12] George Herbert, "The Flower", *The Works of George Herbert*, ed. F. E. Hutchinson (Oxford, 1941), p. 166.

primary vehicle, 'Heart', is wholly submerged; 'heart' is vehicle for a secondary tenor, 'soul' (or 'spirit'), which remains unnamed. This secondary metaphor, 'soul–heart', is positive, for the two terms have so often been equated that they are hardly felt to constitute a metaphor at all. In fact, the emblematic quality of 'heart' for 'soul' suggests moribund allegory. Such metonomy is even more 'positive' than 'Garden–face'. Its chief function here is to provide a firmness in naming for the elusive 'soul' so that grounds for the implicit metaphor 'soul–flower' will be evident. The vivid concretions 'shrivel'd' and 'greenesse' are thus prepared for. Since 'soul' is not itself felt as a metaphor, 'soul–heart' is a submerged, positive, simple metaphor. Its purpose is to make the basic metaphor, 'heart–flower', more positive than it would otherwise be.

The positive quality of 'soul–heart' does not wholly obtain for the basic metaphor, 'heart–flower', for Herbert is not unaware of the distinction between man and plant; repulsions which are not wholly muted are present. A flower must automatically respond to seasonal rhythms; man has consciousness and a degree of free-will. But since Herbert insists that his heart is a flower – the grounds for the shift being 'God's creations' and mutability – there is a basic tension. The old paradox of free will and God's providence is present, though the effect of the metaphor is an emphasis upon providence and a denigration of free-will.

'Heart–flower' may be catalogued as a surface, complex metaphor whose tenor, 'heart', is itself the vehicle of a submerged, simple, positive metaphor. The polarity which emerges is basically positive since it is their similarities which Herbert emphasizes, though there are sufficiently strong repulsions to produce a degree of tension. The net effect is closer to 'garden–face' than to 'busy old fool', more of grace than wit, yet if all repulsions are muted, the metaphor goes flat.

A third metaphor, from Donne's "Goodfriday, 1613", works in a similar fashion, but its effect is negative, rather than positive:

> What a death were it then to see God dye? . . .
> It made his footstoole crack, and the Sunne winke.[13]

'His footstoole' is the vehicle of a submerged metaphor whose tenor is available to the reader by two means: the notion of the earth as God's footstool is familiar enough so that it may be supplied by memory; the

---

[13] John Donne, "Goodfriday, 1613, Riding Westward", *The Poems of John Donne*, ed. H. J. C. Grierson (Oxford, 1912), I, p. 336.

No more shall you returne to it alone,
It nourseth sadnesse, and your bodies print,
Like to a grave, the yielding downe doth dint;
    You and your other you meet there anon;
    Put forth, put forth that warme balme-breathing thigh,
Which when next time you in these sheets wil smother,
    There it must meet another,
       Which never was, but must be, oft, more nigh;
Come glad from thence, goe gladder then you came,
To day put on perfection, and a womans name.

[II]

Daughters of London, you which bee
Our Golden Mines, and furnish'd Treasurie,
    You which are Angels, yet still bring with you
Thousands of Angels on your mariage daies,
Help with your presence and devise to praise
    These rites, which also unto you grow due;
    Conceitedly dresse her, and be assign'd
By you, fit place for every flower and jewell,
    Make her for love fit fewell
       As gay as Flora, and as rich as Inde;
So may shee faire, rich, glad, and in nothing lame,
To day put on perfection, and a womans name.

[III]

And you frolique Patricians,
Sonns of these Senators wealths deep oceans,
    Ye painted courtiers, barrels of others wits,
Yee country men, who but your beasts love none,
Yee of whose fellowships whereof hee's one,
    Of study and play made strange Hermaphrodits,
    Here shine; This bridegroom to the Temple bring.
Loe, in yon path which store of straw'd flowers graceth,
    The sober virgin paceth;
       Except my sight faile, 'tis no other thing;
Weep not nor blush, here is no griefe nor shame,
To day put on perfection, and a womans name.

[IV]

Thy two-leav'd gates faire Temple unfold,
And these two in thy sacred bosome hold,
    Till, mystically joyn'd, but one they bee;
Then may thy lean and hunger-starved wombe
Long time expect their bodies and their tombe,
    Long after their owne parents fatten thee.

All elder claimes, and all cold barrennesse,
All yeelding to new loves bee far for ever,
   Which might these two dissever,
      All wayes all th'other may each one possesse;
For, the best Bride, best worthy of praise and fame
To day puts on perfection, and a womans name.

[V]

Oh winter dayes bring much delight,
Not for themselves, but for they soon bring night;
   Other sweets wait thee then these diverse meats,
Other disports then dancing jollities,
Other love tricks then glancing with the eyes,
   But that the Sun still in our halfe Spheare sweates;
   Hee flies in winter, but he now stands still.
Yet shadowes turne; Noone point he hath attain'd,
   His steeds nill bee restrain'd,
      But gallop lively downe the Westerne hill;
Thou shalt, when he hath runne the worlds half frame,
To night put on perfection. and a womans name.

[VI]

The amorous evening starre is rose,
Why then should not our amorous starre inclose
   Her selfe in her wish'd bed? Release your strings
Musicians, and dancers take some truce
With these your pleasing labours, for great use
   As much wearinesse as perfection brings;
      You, and not only you, but all toyl'd beasts
Rest duly; at night all their toyles are dispensed;
But in their beds commenced
   Are other labours, and more dainty feasts;
She goes a maid, who, least she turne the same,
To night puts on perfection, and a womans name.

[VII]

Thy virgins girdle now untie,
And in thy nuptiall bed (loves altar) lye
   A pleasing sacrifice; now dispossesse
Thee of these chaines and robes which were put on
T'adorne the day, not thee; for thou, alone,
   Like vertue'and truth, art best in nakednesse;
   This bed is onely to virginitie
A grave, but, to a better state, a cradle;
Till now thou wast but able
   To be what now thou art; then that by thee

No more be said, *I may be*, but, *I am*,
To night put on perfection, and a womans name.

[VIII]

Even like a faithfull man content,
That this life for a better should be spent,
  So, shee a mothers rich stile doth preferre,
And at the Bridegroomes wish'd approach doth lye,
Like an appointed lambe, when tenderly
    The priest comes on his knees t'embowell her;
      Now sleep or watch with more joy; and O light
Of heaven, to morrow rise thou hot, and early;
This sun will love so dearely
      Her rest, that long, long we shall want her sight;
Wonders are wrought, for she which had no maime,
To night puts on perfection, and a womans name.

The eight stanzas of John Donne's "Epithalamion made at Lincolnes Inne" follow the pattern of the conventional epithalamion almost perfectly. The bride is awakened (I) and dressed (II). The marriage ceremony takes place, the couple is wished long and happy life (IV). There is a lament that bed time is so long in coming (V). The entertainers at the wedding feast are dismissed (VI). The bride undresses and goes to bed (VII). The groom comes to possess her, and the members of the wedding party speculate as to how late the two will sleep the next morning (VIII). There is an incremental refrain which echoes graceful praise at the end of each stanza. But the poem is very unusual. Rather than celebrating the marriage with praise and optimism, it names flaws in the bride, the groom, the bride's maids and the groom's men, the ceremony, and finally in the consumation of the marriage, with the indelicate, masked, precision of a truly feminine malice. It is quite likely that such an assertion will seem very forced to one meeting the poem for the first time, and it must be added that Donne maintains the possibility of a conventional reading with remarkable skill. The satirical attitude is conveyed by means of metaphorical implications, rather than by overt statement. It is to a discovery of such metaphorical motions that attention will now be turned.

Donne's poem presents a number of problems which are instructive. Since epithalamions are occasional, the contribution of historical scholarship is very much in order. Once it is realized that the students at Lincolnes Inne were not allowed to marry, that Donne did not include the poem in the collection he was making in 1614, and that the entertainment of the young men at the inns frequently took the form of buffoonery and burlesque of serious genres, it is possible to conceive of the epithalamion as broadly satiric. Perhaps it was written for a mock wedding in which the 'bride' would be a man, dressed to impersonate a maid.[15] But all this is to go outside the poem in order to supplement its objective correlatives. No one is likely to deny that biographical and historical facts should be incorporated into a reader's sensibility so as to improve the chances for communication between reader and poet. But to turn to such facts AS THE SOLUTION is to indite the poet or the reader, or both, for not accomplishing AESTHETIC communication.

If the poem is successful, the broadly satiric reading should arise, not from Donne's biography, but from the poem itself. As cultural norms evolve and as the code of language changes, the *sub specie aeternitatis* quality of a poem is reduced, but that reduction is to be regretted. Whenever possible, the appeal should be to the cultural object, not to its historical milieu. One looks at the answers at the back of the book only after having failed to work the problem, or in order to check his results. There is, in the case of the Lincolnes Inne epithalamion, ample evidence for a broadly satiric reading in the structure of its metaphoric action. Further, it is wise to assume that major poets are seldom the authors of purely occasional poems, regardless of their 'intent'. An approach to the poem through a grammar of metaphor reveals statements about the human condition which an 'occasional' reading – whether as satiric or as flattery – fails to discover.

For the moment, let us set aside historical evidence and read the poem *sub specie aeternitatis*. It might be more accurate to say that historical elements will be used, but only as a last resort, historical answers. Donne's persona is perhaps a rejected lover celebrating the marriage of the woman who rejected him, or perhaps he is a friend of the groom who sees his companion marrying unsuitably. The greatest joy of the kind of malice which I posit for the persona is to have the principals accept compliments at face value while bystanders gleefully perceive the double mocking: praise which is insult, phrased so that it must, on the surface, be accepted as praise. Neither the bride nor the groom can quite be sure that the speaker is malicious. Since innuendoes are typical of boistrous marriage celebrations, the speaker may be

---

[15] The historical evidence for reading the poem as broadly satirical is set forth by David Novarr in "Donne's 'Epithalamion Made at Lincoln's Inn': Context and Date", *RES*, VII (1956), 250-263. Novarr's contention that the poem resulted from a mock wedding limits the complexity of his response by making too adamant a connection between the poem and its source. He does, however, isolate a number of 'negative' metaphors in support of his thesis.

simply a bit crude in his choice of images. But actually a clever and systematic manipulation of negative and positive metaphors accomplishes broad satire while maintaining a decorus surface. We have seen this process in operation to opposite effect in Donne's lines on the crucifixion, but rather than moving from heterogeneity to qualified unity as in "Goodfriday, 1613", the epithalamion moves from unity almost to heterogeneity. The satiric effect is achieved by negative metaphors, but the tension of the poem is the result of contrasts between negative and positive possibilities. Both must be recognized if the full quality of the poem is to be felt.

Stanza I begins conventionally enough. The bride is to leave the bed in which she has slept alone for the last time. At first the poet seems to be suggesting a 'death' for the bride which is very much to be desired: by experiencing the 'little death' in the consumation of marriage she will deal a death blow to her virgin state. This reading of 'death' is spelled out in Stanza VII, and the reader must be fully aware of such a positive reading. But the idea is conveyed by imagery which also suggests that her 'death' is less in keeping with a happy wedding. The bed 'nourseth sadnesse', and the indentation left by the bride's body is 'like to a grave'. The first of these images is a surface, positive, complex metaphor. The bed is a nurse whose child is sorrow. The metaphor is strange only because it appears in an epithalamion in which more cheerful imagery might be expected.[16] The second image works in much the same fashion. The bed as a grave is surface and simple, and though it is considerably more negative than 'bed–nurse–child–sadness', the fact that 'bed–grave' is presented as a simile rather than a metaphor encourages the reader to concentrate on positive, rather than negative, relationships. After all, it may be that her imperfect state is to die with the 'completion' which she will find in marriage. At this stage the reader

---

[16] This passage may be contrasted with similar passages from Donne's "An Epithalamion, Or marriage Song on the Lady Elizabeth and Count Palatine being married on St. Valentines day":

> Up then faire Phoenix Bride, frustrate the Sunne
>   Thy selfe from thine affection
>   Takest warmth enough, and from thine eye
> All lesser birds will take their Jollitie.
>   (Grierson, p. 128)

and from Donne's "Epithalamion":

> But now, to Thee, faire Bride, it is some wrong,
>   To thinke thou wert in Bed so long,
>   Since Soone thou lyest downe first, tis fit
> Thou in first rising should'st allow for it.
>   (Grierson, p. 136)

is likely to accept the first stanza as positive; the comparisons are not so flattering as he might expect, but they are not impossible as compliment.

As if to assure the reader that his intent is to praise, Donne notes the bride's 'warme balme-breathing thigh'. I read the tenor as 'thigh' and the vehicle as partially submerged 'animal', qualified by the ambiguous modifiers 'warme' and 'balme'. 'Thigh–animal' is very negative if the intent is to praise the delicate virgin, but the partial submersion of 'animal' allows the reader to accept it as positive, though not without misgivings.[17] 'Bed–nurse–child–sadness', 'bed–grave', and 'animal–thigh' are gathered in the moribund metaphor 'smother'. If the nurse is to smother the child, 'sadness', then the Bed-as-grave is to be sought. But it is not 'child–sadness' which is to be smothered but 'animal–thigh'. Once again Donne disguises the force of the negatives by using a submerged metaphor which is hardly felt to be a metaphor at all; only in the context of the previous comparisons does the literal meaning of 'smother' emerge. The net effect of the first stanza is positive; the reader feels that the images can be made to fit a pattern of compliment. But he is also uncomfortably aware that there seems to be a pattern of awkwardness in the choice of metaphors. Animal sensuality is too near the surface for this stage of the wedding. 'Balme-breathing thigh' is a proper detail for the bedding of the pair, but it is clumsy to note so intimate a detail on the morning of the wedding. At the least, the 'perfection' which she is to put on is thoroughly physical.[18] There is a hint of a negative reading which must be kept in mind.

Stanza II opens with a complex surface metaphor whose polarity is almost perfectly balanced. 'Daughters of London-Golden Mines-furnish'd Treasurie' may be read in two ways.[19] And lest the reader see only the positive reading, Donne finds a pun which insists on both positive and negative: 'Angels'. The spiritual treasure which the bride's friends possess is rudely juxtaposed with their considerable dowry. Donne in explaining the pun suggests that the tangible fortune is their greater attractiveness. The same emphasis is accomplished by the possible *double-entendres* of 'DEVISE to praise' – as if the ladies, like

---

[17]   If a bilingual pun is present, 'Breath' and 'TransPIRE', the image may not have as its tenor 'animal', but even if such is the case, there remains the suggestion that the thigh is some sort of respirating being.

[18]   Jay Halio, "*Perfection* and Elizabethan Ideas of Conception", *English Language Notes*, I (1964), pp. 179-182, illustrates the Aristotelian idea of man as woman's 'perfecter' from Elizabethan literature.

[19]   Grierson finds a similar satiric implication in these opening lines, II, p. 98.

Donne's persona, find it difficult to laud this particular wedding – and the 'rites' which 'grow due'. Such a suspicion of the ladies' virtue would not arise had not Donne alerted the reader with 'mines', 'Treasurie', and 'Angels'. Since to find secondary satiric puns seems forced, perhaps they exist as puns only when the reader refuses conventional readings.

In the same vein, it is curious that the bride's maids should make the bride 'for love fit fewell'. It may be taken to mean that they adorn her in such fashion as to emphasize her delicate virgin grace. But it may also mean that she is dressed to raise the fires of lust in the groom. 'Bride-fuel' is a surface, simple metaphor which is strongly negative. Fuel, after all, is consumed in a fire; after the burning, nothing remains of value. Donne maintains at least the possibility of a positive reading with the qualifier, 'love'. However, the built-in ambivalence of 'love' requires, once again, that the reader keep both possibilities in mind. The comparison seems unflattering, but perhaps the persona is merely clumsy in his praise. To keep this possibility alive, Donne produces two positive images: the bride is 'as gay as Flora, and as rich as Inde'. The two similies, qualified by 'gay' and 'rich', suggest that the entire passage should be read as praise. The reader is encouraged to mute the negative qualities which are expressed in previous metaphors, puns, and similes. But lest the reader rest in a positive reading, Donne concludes the stanza with a very awkward compliment; the bride is 'in nothing LAME'. The praise is faint; the compliment left-handed.

Stanza III presents the groom's men as fit companions for the 'maids' of Stanza II. Donne is less careful to suggest possible complimentary readings of the descriptive images. The positive, surface, simple metaphor, 'groom's men-patricians', is made negative by the qualifier 'frolique'. The initial metaphor is made complex by the four succeeding metaphors: 'Senator's sons', 'courtiers', 'wits', and 'country men' are vehicles for the same tenor – 'groom's men'. Each is qualified in such a way as to turn apparent compliment into insult. The third stage of complexity is particularly interesting. The men are 'barrels' – a very negative metaphor. The qualification 'of others wits', rather than softening the insult, actually adds to it. Here, then, is a thoroughly negative image which is reinforced by a suggestion of animality. The groom's men, who are very like the groom, 'love' none but beasts. The lusty aspect of love's 'fit fewell' is emphasized, and the animal imagery of Stanzas VI and VIII is anticipated. The suggested perversion of 'animal loves' is continued in the complicated image 'Of study and play made strange Hermaphrodits'. If the metaphor is 'groom's men–her-

maphrodits', and if the 'of' means 'by', the groom's men, and by implication the groom, are unfit for marriage. If it is the groom's men who
have produced 'strange hermaphrodits' by mixing study and pleasure,
the image is less vicious, though the hint of perversion remains. In
either case, the concluding metaphor, submerged partially in 'shine'
casts an unnatural light on the marriage. At best the groom's men
reflect others' light, at worst they are false-fires, and it is they who
guide the groom to the temple.

After such a structure of negatives, Donne returns to the bride with
conventional images of praise. The path upon which 'the sober virgin
paceth' is graced by 'straw'd flowers'. The reader initially takes 'bride-
virgin' to be a description, not a metaphor, but the line 'Except my
sight faile, 'tis no other thing' suggests that 'virgin' is the vehicle to the
tenor 'bride' and raises the possibility that the metaphor is a negative
one. The persona seems to say, "She LOOKS like a virgin, but. . . ." The
stanza concludes with the same device employed at the end of Stanza II.
That the bride must be reassured that she need not weep for grief nor
blush for shame at her approaching marriage raises possibilities which
would not have otherwise occurred to the reader. Still, brides are supposed to blush and weep; the ambivalence remains.

The wedding which is described in Stanza IV appears at first to be
as delicate as one could wish. The 'two-leav'd gates' 'unfold', and the
bride and groom are 'mystically joyn'd' in the 'sacred bosome' of the
'Temple'. The delicate vegetable suggestion of leaves unfolding shifts
to the animal 'bosome'. The 'joining' is implicitly physical, and the
'two-leav'd gates' of the 'Temple' may be read as anatomical. Such a
reading is supported by the heavily physical imagery of previous
stanzas; even so, one may accept, for the moment, a complimentary
reading. Yet at the same time he must maintain the possibility that
future images will cause him to come back to Stanza IV to recover the
negative reading. The anatomical suggestions are emphasized in the
'good wishes' which the poet gives the bride and groom. The crypt of
the church is a 'hunger-starved wombe' which will ultimately be sated
with the bodies of the happy pair. In rapid succession the poet names
the conventional subjects for good wishes, but the emphasis is on all
the wrong things. He brings up the events and conditions least suitable
for nuptial wishes: the death of parents, the existence of previous loves,
the possibility of sterility, and the danger of future infidelity. The implication is that the bride has had a lover, is now barren, and will
cuckold her husband when the occasion arises. In such a context the

wish that 'All wayes all th'other may each one possess' is thoroughly physical, if not lewd, and the praise of the bride as 'best worthy of praise and fame' is archly perfunctory.

Stanza V presents the conventional wish that the sun would set so that the couple may go to bed, but the imagery is coarsely physical. The wish for winter is an insult – winter may have long nights, but it is also the time of 'cold barrenesse'. The 'sweets' of the marriage bed are like the 'diverse meats' of the wedding feast, the dance of love like the wedding dance, and skill in love-making (which the bride should not yet possess) like flirting eyes. The three images are inverted metaphors; rather than saying x is y, Donne says x is not y. He protests too much. If the two are not alike, why spend so much time on denials? In saying that the 'sweets' of the marriage bed are 'other' than the diverse meats of a feast, he suggests that the two might be mistaken for each other. 'Sweets–diverse meats' is a surface, complex metaphor whose tenor is the vehicle of another metaphor: 'sex–sweets'. The polarity of the complex is strongly negative. It is one thing to think of sex as 'sweet'; it is quite another to equate such sweetness with the taste of meats. Of course if the poem were straightforward satire, the polarity would be appropriate; that which is impossible as praise may be very fine insult.

That the sun is 'sweating' recalls the animal imagery of the previous stanzas and taints the identification of the bride as the sun which is to come in Stanza VIII. The physical suggestion of sweat is underlined by the sun's unrestrainable 'steeds' who gallop 'lively downe the Westerne hill'. The diction is sharply Freudian. At the least the poet suggests the 'beast with two backs', and the effect is akin to Iago's lewd torturing of Brabantio in the opening of *Othello*. The accuracy of the tenor is undisputable, but the choice of vehicle is malicious.

The first half of Stanza VI is conventional praise in positive terms. 'Amorous evening starre' (Venus) is almost a dead metaphor; Donne awakens it by calling the bride 'our amorous starre', our earthly Venus. Though the plural 'our' might be questioned, the net effect is complimentary, at least on a first reading. The musicians are told to release their strings – apparently a simple command, but the breaking of the line after 'strings' suggests that it is the bride's strings which are to be released. This hinted identification makes the admonition 'great use / As much wearinesse as perfection brings' apply to the entertainment to be provided by the bride as well as that supplied by the musicians and dancers. The entertainers, all three, are then equated with 'all toyl'd beasts' – again reviving the animal motif. That the beasts 'in their beds'

commence 'more dainty feasts' recalls the 'sex–sweets–meats' of Stanza
V. The compliments of the opening lines of Stanza VI are thus inverted.
It is in appetite that the bride is like Venus; her 'labours' are as prac-
ticed as the musicians' fingering and the dancers' gyrations and as
beastial as those of draft animals. Donne is here working almost entirely with suspended metaphors. Only the third and the eleventh lines
of the stanza name the tenor 'bride'. The first three vehicles, 'star',
'musician', and 'dancer' may be read as positive, but the fourth vehicle,
'beast', is so negative as to force the reader to reject it altogether, or to
give a negative reading to the entire cluster.

The pattern of alternation between negative and positive which has
been noted thus far is accomplished largely by contrasts within single
stanzas. In the two stanzas which bring the poem to its climax, a larger
pattern is evident. The two motifs – 'death' and 'animal sensuality' –
are interwoven with the pagan religious imagery first suggested in
Stanza IV. There is an alternation of negatives and positives in both
stanzas, but the two stanzas themselves form a larger pattern of antithesis.

Stanza VII beds the bride. The metaphor of line two, 'bed-altar',
seems at first to be negative, but the qualifiers 'nuptiall' and 'loves'
insist that the metaphor is positive, since both are taken from the same,
positive frame of reference. The notion of the bed as altar suggests a
sacrifice, and the 'virgin' of line one is the obvious choice. The reader
is to accept the conceit as laudatory, but he should note the pagan
quality. 'Bride–sacrifice' is surface, simple and (considered as other
than a moribund metaphor) very negative – just how negative Donne
makes clear in Stanza VIII. The 'chaines' which the bride must shed
are literally her ornaments, but within the context of 'bed–altar–bride–
sacrifice' they suggest the chains which bind an unwilling sacrificial
victim. The play on chains is negative, but the 'robes' which follow ask
the reader to ignore the repulsions between chains of gold and chains
of iron. Similarly, the difference between 'naked truth' and 'naked bride'
is equally obvious, but Donne lessens the negative effect by making the
simile 'Bride-virtue and truth', with 'nakednesse' present only as the
grounds for the shift. The negative metaphor from Stanza I, 'bed-
grave', is repeated, but its repulsions are explained away. It is 'virginitie'
which dies, and a 'better state' which is born. One is reminded of the
Wife of Bath's arguments – even if they are accepted there remains the
gat-toothed grin. The Aristotelian idea of potential and realized state
is surrounded by sensual imagery. Although Donne does not say what

she no longer 'may bee' but is, the reader is very likely to read the realization of self which the bride is to achieve as a good thing. Of course it
is still possible to suggest that the problem is one of reality versus appearance: now, she is NOT a virgin; earlier there was room for argument.
Still, the idea of potential state suggests that 'may be' be read as 'about
to be' rather than as 'perhaps'. Despite the negative possibilities, the
effect of Stanza VII is primarily positive; Donne gives the reader ample
opportunity to mute disparate implications. Stanza VII is perhaps the
most positive stanza in the poem. Were it read separately, it must be
read as conceited flattery.

Stanza VII is positive in spite of negative elements; Stanza VIII is
negative in spite of several positive images. It divides exactly in the
middle. The first half is positive, the second half negative. The bride is
'like a faithfull man'; the disparities in 'bride–man' are muted by the
simile – just as in the famous 'As virtuous men passe mildly away'. The
same device is employed three lines later: she is 'Like an appointed
lambe'. The enormities of the comparison are for the moment muted.
Once again the breaking of the line is significant: 'when tenderly / The
priest comes on his knees t'embowell her'. The shock of the second line
is heightened by the gentleness of the previous line; 'tender lamb' and
'embowell' are worlds apart, yet the logic of the comparison (begun in
Stanza VII) insists that such must be the fate of a lamb upon an altar.

The metaphoric complexity of the last half of Stanza VIII is aston-
ishing. Donne begins with a simile: she is like a lamb. The reader is
invited to discover similarities between a bedded bride and a lamb
about to be sacrificed. Such similarities exist on the metaphysical level,
but the exploration of the simile which follows is vividly physical. The
bridegroom is LIKE a priest, but the like is not repeated and so the
simile moves toward metaphor. The praying priest and the preying
bridegroom are both upon their knees, but the equation contrasts eros
and agape, rather than unifying them. The master-stroke of the poem is
the use of 'embowell'. The word's primary meaning is 'eviscerate', and
the NED lists two contemporary contexts: to remove the bowels as an
extreme punishment for a criminal, or to remove the bowels preparatory
to embalming. In the context of a hunt, slain animals are 'embowelled'
before they are cut up for food. Thus the primary meaning of 'embowell' gathers the negative implications of previous metaphors: cruelty,
animalism, death, barrenness. There is, of course, specific ground for
metaphorical shift, but the ways in which the male organ is like a knife
are just clear enough to avoid heterogeneity in the image. If one suc-

ceeds in muting the violence of negative relationships and makes the maidenhead synecdochical for bowels, the bridegroom's function may be thought of as evisceration, but such a reading strains the feeble grounds for shift beyond reason. If 'embowell' means 'eviscerate', Donne has created a very nearly perfect negative metaphor.

But 'embowell' has a secondary meaning current in Donne's time which he showed his awareness of by use in a sermon. It may mean to fill the bowels. If such is here the case, the bridegroom's function is not only the Aristotelian completion of the woman, but also a literal filling on the wedding night which is to be extended through the gestation period of a child. If this is Donne's meaning, the sacrifice of the bride is both practical and in keeping with God's command to multiply. Such a positive reading of 'embowell' ignores the premise of the simile and so violates its context. It is impossible (or monstrous) to imagine the priest filling the bowels of a sacrificial lamb. To read the entire simile in the light of the secondary meaning of 'embowell' is to develop the groomsmen's love of animals (Stanza III) beyond warrant. Perhaps it is better to read 'embowell' as a pun-metaphor, inclusive but negative. Two meanings are available from the single word, and they conflict. The primary meaning is relevant to the satirical movement which it in part establishes. The secondary meaning is smuggled in as relevant to the non-satiric context. The two meanings, juxtaposed, result in a metaphor so negative as to constitute almost a paradox. The play on 'embowell', so read, is the entire poem in miniature.

Throughout the poem the reader has been asked to keep two readings in mind: a positive reading which mutes disparities and so is complimentary, and a negative reading which notes incongruities and so is satirical. The final stanza signals that it is the negative reading which is to predominate, but without sacrificing the positive. The positive quality of Stanza VII has been a false clue, serving only to heighten the effect of the violent disparities revealed by the primary meaning of 'embowell'. The negative reading is thus the tenor; the positive reading its vehicle. The anti-climax of the last five lines allows the reader to recover from the disorientation occasioned by the sudden upsetting of balance in favor of the negative. The sun is advised to rise 'hot' and 'early' since the earthly 'Sun', the bride who in the evening was Venus, has 'loved' so 'dearly / Her rest' that it will be late when she 'rises'. The puns are accepted easily, and their negative qualities seem a mild release in the wake of the violence of 'embowell'. The penultimate line, 'Wonders are wrought, for shee which had no MAIME', is a parting shot.

On the positive level, a paradox is present: the maiming (deflowering) of the bride brings her to the perfection of wifehood. But on the negative level it is hardly flattering to note that a bride to be is not maimed. Faint praise indeed. The final line, the refrain which has seemed throughout the poem to be on the safe ground of learned compliment is now suspect. 'Puts on' now suggests affectation, and to take the name of woman without possessing the virtues which should accompany it is exactly what a full reading of the negative elements in the poem suggests the bride's action to be.

Donne's "Epithalamion made at Lincolnes Inne" is an extreme case. The reader is not often asked to keep in mind alternative and contradictory readings for such a long time, but the essence of metaphysical metaphor is here very plain. Were the reader asked to ignore the negative qualities of Donne's imagery, the epithalamion would seem to be largely an exercise in bad taste; the reader can hardly be expected to mute so many repulsions with so little help from the poet. On the other hand, if he ignores the positives, the tension which exists in the duple reading disappears; Donne would be merely spewing hate. Metaphysical metaphor demands a great deal of the reader. Not only must he, as in all metaphor, be aware of the tension which exists in each image, but he must store contradictory readings so that when the poem is finished he can combine the two, juxtapose the reading based upon muted imagery with the reading produced by his awareness of negatives. The result is metaphor in a large sense. He can then decide whether the negative or the positive meaning is the tenor and what modifications the vehicle reading achieves. The combination of the two is more than their simple total. In metaphysical poetry the idea of duple-unity is applicable not only to individual images, but to the poem as a whole. It well may be that the attractiveness of Donne's poetry lies in his ability to see unity in disparity without sacrificing the disparity. "Epithalamion made at Lincolnes Inne" neither denies paradox nor explains it away. After all, the persona must have greatly loved the bride (or the groom) to have felt the need to destroy her so utterly with compliments. Who would not trade places with Ares trapped in Hephaestus' net?

V

AFTERWORD: THEMATICS,
THE LOCATION OF VERBAL ART

> One gift alone of all they bring I prize.
> Slender its ankles, more graceful than a spear.
> Round in the haunch as bronze that holds the wine.
> And on its belly, down more delicate than floss.
> Above the whisp of twisted silk, translucent cones
> Cool, like gold shaping at leisure in spring rain.
> Below, a forge and tempering bath too tender
> For my calloused hands to wield.
> Useless Aphrodite, unless a pattern for my golden
> I, the maker.   Slaves.
> Yet I glory,
> When they look at her.
>
> From "Hephaestus Cuckold"

A. THEMATICS

The readings which conclude Chapter Four are, I think, a fair sample
of what New Criticism can accomplish. The advantages are so obvious
that it is hard to conceive of a time when the study of literature will
shake off the basic commitments asserted: close reading, fidelity to the
text, the integrity of a poem, a deep interest in imagery, and a heroic
insistence that poetry is, in some degree, *sub specie aeternitatis*. Since
the assembling of historical, biographical data now is vastly simplified
by computer technology, it seems unlikely that the best critical minds
of the future will return to historicism. Myth criticism, except in the
hands of a few, imposes the universal in such a way as to blur the sharp
edge of the individual poem. And the dozens of hyphenated criticisms
spawned by inter-disciplinary studies too often sprawl between stools.
Perhaps the renewed interest in genre study and the amorphous attitudes of 'structuralism'[1] may develop a useful syncretism.

[1] Peter Caws, "What is Structuralism", *Partisan Review*, XXXV (1968), 75-91,
attempts to define the French Structuralist movement.

But the problems we have noted in the New Criticism remain: most basically, the seemingly unavoidable dualism of objective and subjective. In another form this problem may be stated as the inviolability of the work of art, its 'organicism', which must at every point be breached if the reader is to gain access to the poem. Certainly the world of art is a secondary universe which obeys its own laws, but without bridges to our world of experience, it can neither be constructed nor visited. Or is it perhaps that art is not so alien as, judging by the New Critics, might be supposed? Perhaps a poem rises from the same conditions and structures which produce cultural objects as diverse as religion and technology. Now that the disparities between art and science, between the expressions of poetry and the propositions of philosophy, have been granted, now that we have rejected (hopefully) the idea of poetry as substitute religion, it may be useful to go back to discover, not differences, but similarities in cultural objects.

But before turning back to questions so basic as to seem primarily demands for emotional reassurance, we may look at a more recent book by the most promising of the 'grandsons' treated in Chapter Three. The boundless energy and quick mind of Murray Krieger show, in *The Tragic Vision*,[2] exactly why we cannot simply go on from the New Critics. Despite his agressive style, the book is not a confident one. Most of the crucial aesthetic pronouncements are phrased as questions, and the questions are not always rhetorical. The perspective of the last four chapters of our study may indicate both why *The Tragic Vision* came to be written and why it is, in aesthetic theory, unsatisfactory.

'Thematics', as Krieger calls his method, is a perfectly logical outgrowth of New Criticism. The materials upon which Thematics is to operate are the novels equivalent to metaphysical poetry, without the security of the Renaissance world-view. But whereas the 'manichaean' tensions of Donne are subordinated to the possibility of unitive visions, and whereas the New Critics confine their treatment of ambiguity to poetry, Krieger deals with the 'existential' novel and suggests that its crises are both aesthetic and philosophical. This must be so, of course, if he is to treat thematically those novels which lend themselves readily to existential analysis, but the application of tools which seemed fairly precise when employed on poetic imagery to questions of ontology and existence is an invitation to imprecision.

The tensions which he discovers are, despite his denials, philosoph-

[2] Murray Krieger, *The Tragic Vision: Variations on a Theme in Literary Interpretation* (Chicago, 1966). First published in 1960.

ical. Man, living in chaotic experience, inevitably constructs ordered systems upon which to base his actions. At the extremity of crisis, the ordered (hence benevolent) system fails, and he passes through Manicheanism to diabolism, thus acknowledging a new set of absolutes, this time destructive and demoniac, rather than angelic and unitive. Krieger rules the 'leap of faith' as out of bounds for literature and is thus left with limited alternatives. The first is the tragic vision: the final realization that order does not exist, that all 'systems' and values are simply pragmatic. The second is a refusal to confront the extreme, without yet denying its reality. The third, which he favors, sounds, in part at least, like a description by a New Critic of metaphor, transferred to existentialism:

Can we not, then, get at all beyond tension? If not, how are we to be assured that the tension, with its unyielding dualism, will hold the work together through the delicate poise it creates among its oppositions and not split it assunder through a tug of war among them?

The answer for both metaphor and existence is that we cannot. With metaphor we may be content to describe the reconciliation, the split, or the tension without a moral concern for its philosophical value. But once philosophy has been introduced, moral judgments are inevitable.

The power of the tragic vision is very clear, but the problem of an 'organic', 'unique contextual system', becomes severe. Krieger, at moments, limits the wholeness to the aesthetic form: while the materials of the poem come from the existential world, the evolution of aesthetic form makes poetry *sui generis*. But his theoretical attitude comes out most clearly (perhaps unconsciously) when at the end of *The Tragic Vision* he sums up the value of the existential challenge treated in art:

[The reader], not fatally challenged ... has yet learned vicariously to see extremity as the necessary and most instructive vision, the illusion ... , that which creates reality for us by forcing us to see it as we never dare to outside of art because in art we think it is appearance only. For secure in what we take to be more aesthetic illusion, we plunge into the risk of art ... that which terrifies even as it returns us, newly sound and justified, to our middle ... existences chastened by extremity and taking up the order in our lives with tender hands that now know its delusiveness and its fragile, unsubstantial prospects. (pages 256-257)

This is very like the power which I have claimed for genuine simultaneity as it resists the unifying efforts of emotion and mind. But it is only one (and not the most common) result of aesthetic experience. The idea that art fools us into thinking was suggested by Empson and must be sometimes true, but I would resist making such trickery a central justification.

Krieger's problem still seems to be that noted in *The New Apologists*. There he puzzled over the ability of a pot, a rug, a poem, and a sunset to produce reactions each of which seems to be aesthetic, and decided, hurriedly, that either 'someone' gave those objects aesthetic form, or that the perceiver simply imposed his aesthetic habits on nonaesthetic materials. In such bald form, this seems to be Richards' third level of aesthetic sophistication: a tertiary quality, aesthetic in itself, resides in the artifact. By now it should be clear that this will not do. At best such an answer provokes a search for an all-important aesthetic structure. It is not so much wrong as incomplete. And anyway, Krieger's analysis of "The Cannonization" indicated that he had solved the problem practically, if not in theory.

But the problem of organic form will not simply go away. The practical critic may avoid it almost indefinitely, but eventually theory must face the paradox in an attempt to discover a coherent solution. The best we should hope for is a series of successive approximations, but such a realization must not lead to the leap of non-faith. Neither Platonic, nor angelic, nor demoniac, nor Manichean, the critic must eternally return to the insoluble question. Criticism, like poetry, is a process, not a conclusion.

B. THE LOCATION OF VERBAL ART

Northrop Frye in the "Polemical Introduction' to *Anatomy of Criticism*[3] makes an absolute distinction between the study of criticism and the study of literature. The first task of the critic, says Frye, is to establish a solid theoretical foundation. An astronomer does not study the stars, he studies astronomy. He studies a system for approaching phenomena, not the phenomena directly. It is only after having mastered the discipline that he looks directly at the stars AS AN ASTRONOMER, and his perceptions are guided by that discipline. Nevertheless the construction of a systematic approach presupposes an order and intelligibility in nature. If that order were totally perceived, astronomy would no longer be necessary. The astronomer constructs a model of the universe, a model which is dynamic and therefore expands to encompass new data and contracts to expel data which has been super-

[3] Northrop Frye, *Anatomy of Criticism* (Princeton, 1957).

seded. The model approaches all possible observations, but does not equal them unless the universe is to become static. The ratio of circumference to radius is expressed in an infinite-sided polygon. The circle itself escapes the system. Frye insists that the distinction between the study of criticism and the study of literature is similar and must be maintained:

.... criticism, if a science, must be totally intelligible, but literature, as the order of words which makes the science possible, is, so far as we know, an inexhaustible source of new critical discoveries, and would be even if new works of literature ceased to be written. If so, then the search for a limiting principle in literature in order to discourage the development of criticism is mistaken. The absurd quantum formula of criticism, the assertion that the critic should confine himself to "getting out" of a poem exactly what the poet may vaguely be assumed to have been aware of "putting in," is one of the many slovenly illiteracies that the absence of systematic criticism has allowed to grow up. (page 17)

The critic's task, according to Frye, is to construct ever more accurate, coherent systems which are superseded by other systems as the model approximates all possible instances of verbal art. But an awareness of the dynamic quality of verbal art makes it clear that any conceiveable system will be only an approximation. Such an attitude balances nicely between critical despair and the equal error of optimism. The critic can do a great deal; he cannot 'solve' the problem.

Although we can never really begin at the beginning, we need to go back to first things. It is axiomatic that before an object can be described and classified it must first be located. Thus the primary task of critical theory should be to discover where verbal art exists – to place it within the phenomenological frame. René Wellek's definition is a convenient starting point in that it is both eclectic and well-known. Since Wellek's studies impinge on a number of disciplines, he is able to bring together disparate insights and so allow a beginning other than ab ovo. We may now investigate in some detail the implications of Wellek's definition of verbal art which was quoted in the preface to this study as a prediction of the ultimate conclusions of the New Critics:

The work of [verbal] art ... appears as an object of knowledge sui generis which has a special ontological status. It is neither real (like a statue) nor mental (like the experience of light or pain) nor ideal (like a triangle). It is a system of norms of ideal concepts which are intersubjective. They must be assumed to exist in collective ideology, changing with it, accessible only through individual mental experiences, based on the sound-structure of its sentences. (page 144)

This definition, supported by the chapter which it summarizes, answers the question, "What is verbal art not?" but its positive assertions are less satisfactory. 'Norms', 'ideal concepts', 'intersubjective', 'collective ideology' – with each term it is possible to make a wrong turn, and in so compressed a definition, a false step is fatal. The positive statements are 'assumptions' and so self-justifying. Before accepting or rejecting Wellek's definition, it is necessary to discover just what he is saying. It is possible to reconstruct his meaning from the work of other thinkers, spread over a number of disciplines, each of which is involved in investigating cultural objects. The 'borrowings' I shall make are not specific findings, nor an attempt to make literary criticism into linguistics or anthropology or philosophy, or some other hyphenated discipline, but rather I attempt to discover common denominators in the investigation of similar phenomena. It is inevitable that subtle distinctions, important to each man's chosen discipline, will be blurred, and that I will find likenesses that may seem doubtful. It is not possible in such short space to be 'fair' to either authors or disciplines. Although the list might easily be extended, clarification of Wellek will be sought in the work of a Logical Positivist, an Anthropologist, a Linguist, and a Russian Formalist.

Rudolf Carnap in *The Logical Structure of the World*[4] divides 'objects' (by objects he means identifiable entities and processes) of perception into three large classes: the Physical, the Psychological, and the Cultural. Although he makes provision for other classes, such as the Ideal, his development of the three is sufficient for our purpose. His discussion, like Wellek's is chiefly useful in eliminating verbal art from the domain of both physical and psychological objects and thus breaking out of the dualism of objective and subjective which we have seen constantly frustrating the New Critics. He is able to posit an existence for cultural objects which is neither artifactual nor affective.

Briefly and much simplified, his arguments run thus: Physical Objects are characterized by their occupation of a given space and are discriminated by shape, size, and position. They possess at least one sensory quality – such as color, weight, or temperature. Verbal art as artifact, as the marks on the page, certainly fits this definition, but only in special limited cases need criticism give its primary attention to verbal art as physical object. The degree of physicality of most verbal art is slight, and works which depend heavily on spatial or auditory manipulations for artistic effect are readily identifiable. Generally, the physicality of verbal art is a function of its documentation, rather than of the

4 Rudolf Carnap, *The Logical Structure of the World* (Berkeley, 1967).

art itself. Although it is both unwise and nearly impossible to ignore completely the influence of artifact, the general danger is not that physical elements will be disregarded, but that their effect will be over-rated. The arguments of Richards against thinking of verbal art as artifact which are summarized in Chapter One, above, support Carnap and anticipate Wellek.

Carnap defines Psychological Objects as acts of consciousness and of the unconscious, such as perceptions, representations, feelings, and thoughts. Although physical objects, like psychological objects, are temporally determined, they differ in that psychological objects have no sensory qualities and no spatial determination. There is, of course, the exception evidenced by a clear awareness of odor or pain when no external stimulus is present, but such exceptions are psychological objects in that they are subject-bound and are therefore neither directly communicable nor subject to empirical verification. To anticipate Carnap's argument, just as the documentation of verbal art is a physical object, so too the PERCEPTION of verbal art is psychological. What is to be avoided are two complementary fallacies between which the New Critics alternated: first, the mistaking of documentation for verbal art and so treating poetry as physical, and second, assuming that verbal art is perception and so treating it as psychological object. Wellek muddies the water by positing 'norms' of 'ideal concepts' which are 'intersubjective', after having asserted that verbal art is not 'ideal', and then invites confusion by limiting its accessibility to 'individual mental experiences'. The problem is with terminology, rather than meaning, but the opportunity for confusion can be reduced. As will appear, Carnap's third category, Cultural Objects, is able to make the *sui generis* quality of verbal art clear and at the same time to identify a larger general category to which verbal art belongs.

At this stage it may be objected that since the perception of all objects, psychological, physical, and cultural, occurs only as psychological phenomena, all objects are – at least as they are perceived – to a degree psychological. And that the mode of perception in a very important way influences what is perceived. The truth of such assertions is demonstrated by both Cassierer and McLuhan,[5] but without denying validity, it is possible to set them aside. If an overriding psychological context is posited which (1) contains all objects and (2) is, at least in

---

[5] Both *Understanding Media* and *Language and Myth* are based upon this contention. See *The Gutenberg Galaxy* (Toronto, 1962) for McLuhan's clearest statement, pp. 265-279.

quality, shared by all perceivers, one may concentrate on the differences which exist within that general context. If both assumptions were not true, it would be impossible to agree as to the nature and value of art, or even to communicate at all.

On a different level of objection, the degree of influence which the psychological nature of verbal art exerts may be assigned to a discussion of perception. Carnap's basic distinction lies in empirical verifiability: physical objects, because they are not subject-bound may be so verified, psychological objects, subject-bound, may not empirically be verified.

Carnap's third category, cultural objects, is the province of verbal art. Cultural objects, like psychological objects, are subject-bound, but they are intersubjective – that is, they may continue to exist though individual bearers change. A custom, for example, is not dependent upon the immortality of a specific bearer, though if all bearers perish, such a cultural object no longer exists. Hence we have a distinction between cultural object and ideal object. The notion of a triangle may be arrived at an infinite number of times without communication between bearers; such is not the case for cultural objects. It may seem that Carnap's cultural objects are some sort of combination between physical and psychological; to explore the reasons for insisting that such is not the case, let us turn from the logical positivist to a cultural anthropologist.

Walter Goldschmidt, in *Comparative Functionalism: An Essay in Anthropological Theory*,[6] clarifies the notion of Cultural Object and suggests methods for investigating its nature and function. A cultural object, on the most primitive level, results from an attempt to fulfill a social need. The animal nature of man demands solutions for basic problems: the need for food, shelter, protection, and the nurture of dependent children. Such problems must be solved in relation to prevailing ecology and hence will take a variety of forms which appear radically different but which are functionally similar. Even on the fundamental level, group solutions take on the quality of cultural objects in that they immediately demand sets of conventions governing conduct, conventions of activity which are at first directly related to the satisfaction of basic needs, but which rapidly gain a degree of independent existence. Following a leader who is adept at bear-killing may readily be transferred to following a leader as a sign of respect. The practical

---

[6] Walter Goldschmidt, *Comparative Functionalism: An Essay in Anthropological Theory* (Berkeley, 1966).

response has become a cultural object. Cultural objects, then, may be defined as complexes of norms which result in the proclivity to react conventionally so as to express a social relationship. The practical raising of a visor for military recognition becomes the impractical tipping of a hat. Although the manifestations of a particular cultural object may differ widely, they may usefully be grouped on the basis of function. It is in function that Goldschmidt finds the most useful criteria for description and classification.[7]

The applicability of this insight for verbal art is evidenced in V. Propp's *Morphology of the Folktale*. Propp focuses on the function of elements whose interrelationship provides discriminants for the artistic whole:

The functions of a folktale's dramatis personae must be considered as its basic components; and we must first of all extract them as such. In order to extract them we must, of necessity, define them. Definition must proceed from two points of view. First of all, definition should, in no case, stem from the dramatis persona – the "bearer" of a function. Definition of a function is most often given in the form of a noun expressing an action . . . . Secondly, an action cannot be defined apart from its place in the process of narration. The meaning which a given function has in the process of action must be considered.[8]

In practical terms, this means that folk tales must not be classified into tales about dragons and tales about magic rings, but must be examined to determine the structural relation of their component parts. To oversimplify, a-dragon-carries-off-a-maiden and a-prince-eats-a-poisoned-apple may be the same morpheme. Classification according to function insists that the context of each element be considered, for functions exist only in relation to the context which defines them. Here is Richards' idea of the interinanimation of members of a context developed into a methodology. Propp greatly simplifies the conception of context, and to a lesser degree of function, but useful general principles applied practically are evident.

To return to Carnap: cultural objects exist at moments when they are not being expressed. So long as the psychological inclination exists to react in a particular fashion to a particular stimulus, so long exists the

[7]   It may be that Goldschmidt places himself outside Structuralism as defined by Lévi-Strauss: "form defines itself by opposition to a content which is exterior to it; but structure has no content; it is itself the content, apprehended in a logical organization conceived as a property of the real". Quoted by Caws.
[8]   V. Propp, *Morphology of the Folktale*, translated by Laurence Scott (Philadelphia, 1958), p. 19.

cultural object. During the times between manifestations, cultural objects are latent. This provides a sharp distinction between the cultural
object and its manifestation, and suggests a further distinction between
the two and documentation. A documentation is a permanent physical
object which preserves stimuli which can elicit manifestations of the
cultural object. For verbal art, documentations are the printed page or
recordings of readings. Carnap here provides an answer to the question,
"Where is the poem when it is not being read or heard?" without re-
sorting to artifactualism. Since literary criticism operates primarily on
manifestations based on documentations, it is essential to understand
the relationships which exist between the cultural object and its manifestation and between both and its documentation. For Carnap, the task
of the cultural sciences, of which literary criticism must be a special
and very difficult case, is to provide definitions and discover criteria
for the recognition, description, and classification of cultural objects.

The advantages of the general principles suggested by Carnap, Goldschmidt, and Propp are clear. First of all, it is possible to posit an
existence for verbal art which is neither identical with marks upon a
page nor with the perception of a single individual. Further, the method
of criticism here foreshadowed admits of multiple assaults on the morphological elements of literature, and in its division of verbal art into
Cultural Object, Manifestation, and Documentation, acknowledges the
claims of both objectivists and subjectivists. Such distinctions are not
only theoretically more satisfactory than those of Richards, but they
also offer a plan of attack.

There are of course serious limitations. Carnap feels that the study
of cultural objects should be confined to ascertaining 'facts', excluding
all interpretation and value judgment. He considers 'metaphysical' (*i.e.*
improper) the posing of any question for which there is not at least the
possibility of an empirically verified answer. The literary critic is unlikely to be content with the reductivism and exclusion of logical positivism. Goldschmidt focuses on cultural institutions which are much
broader, less conscious, and more 'basic' than verbal art. His study
makes no provision for the role of individual artist or individual reader.
Literature is both more conscious and more swiftly malleable than the
institutions of which he speaks. Responses to literature are more closely
related to their documentation than is the case with most cultural objects and are at the same time further removed from hypothetically
practical inceptions; they may in fact have no discernible practicality
beyond a dimly perceived 'ordering of impulses' such as posited by I. A.

Richards. Verbal art is both more sophisticated and more 'artificial' than the cultural objects which concern Goldschmidt, but if we realize its reflexive qualities – the 'interinanimation' which exists among verbal object, manifestation, documentation, and perception, it is possible to see in Goldschmidt's and Carnap's Cultural Objects a simplified schema which points in a useful direction. To investigate that direction, we may now turn from the anthropologist to a linguist.

The relationship between cultural objects and their manifestations is illuminated by De Saussure in *Cours de Linguistique Generale*.[9] Without concerning ourselves with the implications for linguistics of Saussurian thought, we may borrow a useful distinction which he makes and apply it functionally to verbal art. *Langue* is the system of language which is spoken by no one but which provides an overriding dynamic model for all specific instances of communication. It is, in Carnap's terms, a Cultural Object. *Parole* is a specific, individual attempt to communicate which makes use of the proclivities established by the cultural norms of *Langue*. In Goldschmidt's terms, *parole* is a manifestation of the Cultural Object, *langue*. The printed page is a documentation of a manifestation which is imprecise enough to constitute stimuli for a wide, though not infinite, variety of future manifestations. These discriminations allow the literary critic to make use of a particular printing, reading, or hearing of a piece of verbal art without committing the 'artifactual fallacy': without asserting that the 'poem' is firmly before him in its essential quality.

Oral documentation must not be confused with performance. Records, tapes, and films are documents; when they are played back, a performance results. The performance of a manifestation frequently serves as stimulus for additional manifestations, manifestations which for affective reasons are not likely to be identical to the manifestation which occasioned the performance. For example: when a poem is read aloud, the reader translates the code of the documentation, manifests it in engrammatic organization and then performs that manifestation by encoding it in sound. The listener is then stimulated by the sound to produce his own manifestation. The distinction between performance and documentation is between a set of stimuli which are unique in time and a set which, because they are physically embodied, may be repeated identically.

Both performance and oral documentation contain stronger *parole* elements than does the printed page. They eliminate spatial considera-

[9] De Saussure, *Cours de Linguistique Generale* (Paris, 1916).

tions (size and clarity of type, arrangement on the page), govern the temporal constituents which in print are at the discretion of the reader, and introduce further stimuli (inflection, stress, juncture, *etc.*) which can only be approximated by the most complicated type font. Generally speaking, a specific oral performance or documentation is closer to a specific manifestation than is printed documentation. The responder to printed documentation is both performer and audience, though these stages do not occur discretely; the responder to oral documentation need not make for himself the translation from documentation to performance as he responds to stimuli by manifesting the cultural object. The importance of such hair-splitting distinctions is to insist that the cultural object is *langue*, that it is dynamic and not to be confused with the static *parole* of either performance or documentation. It must, of course, be added that the cultural object is unavailable except through individual manifestation, but this is not to equate such a manifestation with the cultural object.

But let us return to the structuralist tool provided by Saussurian *langue* and *parole*. If it is remembered that the terms as here used are functional rather than essential, the value of a structuralist approach is evident in the sophistication which it invites in the study of poetic rhythm. If meter, the theoretical pattern of accents, is set in the place of *langue* and prose syntactical patterns of accent are set in the place of *parole*, a description can be made of poetic rhythm which is both more useful and more accurate than that enabled by traditional methods of scansion. For example, the lines:

> So sáying, hér rash hánd in évil hóur
> Forth réaching tó the frúit, she plúcked she eát,

would be marked something like this in traditional scansion. The 'latinate' syntax might well be described and something said of caesura, but little else. 'Ing to' and 'she plucked' are marked as identical elements of rhythm. Formal analysis of the line reveals that such is not the case. 'She plucked' is a very strong iamb because the syntactical stress pattern of subject-verb agrees with the metrical pattern. 'Ing to' represents a conflict between meter and syntax. The syntactical rhythmic function of 'to' is as the first of two unstressed syllables in the prepositional phrase 'to the fruit'. It is only against the *langue* of iambic pentameter that the podic unit 'ing to' emerges. That traditional scansion might see 'Forth' as a secondary accent is an acknowledgment of syntactical influence. A word which violates its usual syntactic placement calls attention to itself and so tends to be stressed. These two examples by no means account for the lines' rhythmic complexity, but they indicate both the method and kind of result which Structuralism provides in the study of meter.

It may be objected that such attention to the 'texture' of poetry is exactly what the New Critics sought. Such is certainly the case, but with rare exceptions the New Critics reach their conclusions by sensibility and resist as reductive any broad system which implies that each case is not unique. It is impossible to reduce Empson's seven types to a coherent system, or even to extract from Tate's touchstones general principles which could be called a theory. A general distaste for logical positivism or even for Richards' struggles for theoretical coherence precluded the general systemization which would have been necessary if a 'school' of criticism were to have emerged from what in the last analysis must be called an island chain of sensibilities.

There were, of course, adequate reasons for resisting the development of a new critical organum. Chief among these was the objective-subjective dilemma. But there are two other complicating factors inherent in the study of verbal art which make systems suspect. The first of these is the importance of unique context. It is impossible to treat elements of a poem discretely without doing considerable violence to the 'discrete' element. For example, the repetition of syntactical pattern in 'she plucked, she eat' affects the rhythm of Milton's line as does the alliteration of 's's'. The meaning of the line interjects horrific emphasis. The contextual symbolism of Eve as flower suggests 'shé Plucked' as a possible inversion: that it is Eve who is plucked, and with her all humanity. Ravening death and foul digestion, the banquet with Raphael, the Platonic lecture on digestive ascension – all affect the rhythm of 'she plucked, she eat'. Clearly the division of rhythm into syntax and meter only scratches the surface of the rhythmic power of those four words. As we have seen, Richards defines the meaning of a word as the total of the missing parts of its context; the same may be said of any morphological element. Verbal art, Cultural Object, is an intensive manifold. No single part can be considered in isolation, because no part is itself when divorced from its context. The New Critics were right; in the hands of a logical positivist structuralism can be both reductive and exclusive. Where, they might ask, is there a system of scansion which would account for the complexity of Milton's rhythmic manifold? And if such a system were devised, would it not be unique to this line and useless or misleading if applied to other lines of Milton, much less to lines by, for example, James Dickey? But so long as the study of criticism, as opposed to literature, is not mistaken for the cultural object, so long as systems are dynamic means toward the end of fuller understanding. Structuralism with its insistence on the primacy of function and context makes the critic more, rather than less, aware of the complexity of verbal art.

The second complicating factor lies in the peculiar relationships among the cultural object, its manifestation, its documentation, and its perception. Carnap's and Goldschmidt's discriminations hold, but are simplistic. In verbal art, there are two separate kinds of manifestation. The first is the creative manifestation of the poet as he produces the poem. This stage is roughly analogous to the relationship between cultural object and manifestation outlined by Goldschmidt, but the poet is in more conscious control of the form which both manifestation and documentation take than is the case when 'society' is the creator and its members the more or less unconscious manifesters and documenters. The poet is not tipping his hat in semi-automatic response. In his creative manifestation he PRODUCES a cultural object, and there is an interplay between the documentation and the creation. The further distinction between composing the poem and the document which is produced is of psychological, rather than critical, interest. Even when changes in manuscripts are available, the critic must intuit the altered manifestation which occurred between one documentation and another. René Wellek dismisses such investigations as 'obstetrical criticism', and with more respect they may be set aside as better suited for psychological investigation of creativity than for criticism.

The second kind of manifestation is that of the reader when confronted with a documentation provided by the poet. Immediately it is obvious that Carnap's and Goldschmidt's order has been reversed. Here it is the documentation which precedes the manifestation. And except in the artificial case of the student and critic, such reader-manifestations do not lead to documentations. If we are to remain with Carnap's conceptions at all, a major sophistication must be made, in somewhat the following manner. A reader has stored in his cultural awareness the elements of poetic communication. These elements range from a knowledge of the language code to awareness of special poetic forms. In theory, the entire cultural system and its normative responses is available to every member of the culture, but in reality no individual possesses all the elements of his culture and each member of a cultural group is in some ways unique. Once again the conceptions of *langue* and *parole* are useful. The 'Cultural heritage' which is in theory available is *langue*, the actual possession by any individual is *parole*. The individual may gain awareness of cultural elements incidentally in the process of living within a group, or he may gain such awareness artificially, by the study of his own or another culture. Since the *langue* of culture is constantly altering, but since the changes are evolutionary rather than absolute, the awareness of particular cultural elements is neither discrete nor static. An analogy may clarify: suppose the theoretically available cultural elements to be written on a blackboard in a dark room. Further suppose the individual awareness to be a flashlight directed upon one section of the blackboard. The direction and width of the beam is determined by the time, place, experience, and education of the individual as well as by his innate intelligence and sensitivity. If we posit an infinite blackboard upon which cultural elements are continually being enscribed, a rough notion of the materials of the cultural *langue* in relation to the *parole* of an individual's awareness may emerge. The function of education is to illuminate a larger and larger section of the blackboard.

The documentation produced by the poet encodes a particular organization of cultural elements. The reader translates that code in the light of his own cultural awareness and so manifests the cultural object. Neither the elements which are combined nor the particular combination nor the response to that combination are identical in separate manifestations, but because of the similarities in education, experience, and being – similarities in heredity and environment – the individual response generally falls within a circle of perception shared by other members of the cultural group. Since that circle is dynamic, but does not change absolutely, verbal art is both a document of its age and *sub specie aeternitatis*.

An attempt may now be made to restate Wellek's definition of verbal art, in the light of the structuralist insights which have been discussed. The creative manifestation of the poet is not, for reasons which have been stated, to be considered here.

Verbal Art is a particular kind of *Cultural Object*. It is not to be confused with *Physical Object* (its *documentation*), nor with *Psychological Object* (its *perception*). It exists latently in the proclivities of a cultural group to respond in an organized fashion to an organized set of stimuli. The elements to be organized and the method of organization exist latently in its documentation, which is a coded form of the creative manifestation of the poet. In order for a perceptual manifestation to occur, the perceiver must possess the code system of the documentation. Both the code and normative responses to it change through cultural and individual experiences, and through time and place. Such changes are evolutionary rather than absolute. Verbal art is thus *dynamic*: both a document of the age in which it was created and *sub specie aeternitatis*.

Doubtless, future critics will find new ways of dealing with verbal art. Hephaestus is the archetype of the literary critic, and despite the absolute failure of his net to catch either the attraction or the pleasure which brings together Aphrodite and Ares, to have exhibited the conjunction of love and war is no mean accomplishment for a cripple. It is time to return to the forge, carrying with us the skill in tempering which the New Critics, in their inevitable failure, have gained.

BIBLIOGRAPHY

Brooks, Cleanth, *Modern Poetry and the Tradition* (Chapel Hill, 1939).
——, *The Well Wrought Urn* (New York, 1947).
——, and Robert Penn Warren, *Understanding Poetry*, 3rd ed. (New York, 1960).
Carnap, Rudolf, *The Logical Structure of the World* (Berkeley, 1967), original publication (Berlin, 1928).
Cassirer, Ernst, *Language and Myth*, trans. Susanne Langer (New York, 1946).
Caws, Peter, "What is Structuralism", *Partisan Review*, XXV (1968), 75-91.
Chatman, Seymour, *A Theory of Meter* (The Hague, 1965).
Ciardi, John, Epigram, *The Poetry Public Letter*, II (1954), 13.
Coleridge, Samuel T., *Biographia Litteraria*, ed. J. Shawcross (London, 1907).
De Saussure, *Cours de Linguistique Generale* (Paris, 1916).
Donne, John, *The Poems of John Donne*, ed. H. J. C. Grierson, 2 vols. (Oxford, 1912).
Elton, William, *A Glossary of the New Criticism* (Chicago, 1948).
Empson, William, *Seven Types of Ambiguity* (London, 1930).
Erlich, Victor, *Russian Formalism*, 2nd ed. (The Hague, 1965).
Foster, Richard, *The New Romantics* (Bloomington, 1962).
Fromm, Erich, D. T. Suzuki, and Richard De Martino, *Zen Buddhism and Psychoanalysis* (New York, 1960).
Frye, Northrop, *Anatomy of Criticism* (Princeton, New Jersey, 1957).
——, "The Archetypes of Literature", *Kenyon Review*, XIII, i (1951), 92-110.
Goldschmidt, Walter, *Comparative Functionalism: An Essay in Anthropological Theory* (Berkeley, 1966).
Halio, Jay, "*Perfection* and Elizabethan Ideas of Conception", *English Language Notes*, I, iii (1964), 179-182.
Henderson, Harold G., *An Introduction to Haiku* (New York, 1958).
Herbert, Edward, *The Poems English and Latin of Edward Lord Herbert of Cherbury*, ed. G. C. Moore Smith (Oxford, 1923).
Hulme, T. E., *Speculations*, ed. Herbert Read (London, 1924).
——, *Further Speculations*, ed. Sam Hynes (Minnesota, 1955).
Krieger, Murray, *The New Apologists for Poetry* (Minneapolis, 1956).
——, *The Tragic Vision* (Chicago, 1966). First published, 1960.
Langer, Susanne K., *Feeling and Form* (New York, 1953).
——, *Philosophy in a New Key* (Cambridge, 1942).
Mason, H. A., "T. E. Hulme by Michael Roberts", review in *Scrutiny*, VII, ii (1938), 215-16.
McLuhan, Marshall, *The Gutenberg Galaxy* (Toronto, 1962).
Miles, Josephine, "Correspondence: More Semantics of Poetry", *Kenyon Review*, II, iv (1940), 502-507.
Monk, Samuel Holt, "The Pride of Lemuel Gulliver", *Sewanee Review*, LXIII, i (1955), 48-71.

Novarr, David, "Donne's 'Epithalamion Made at Lincoln's Inn': Context and Date", *RES*, VII (1956), 250-263.

Ong, Walter, Jr., "The Meaning of the 'New Criticism' ", *The Modern Schoolman*, XX (1943), 192-209.

Propp, V., *Morphology of the Folktale*, translated by Laurence Scott (Philadelphia, 1958).

Ransom, John Crowe, "The Concrete Universal", *Kenyon Review*, XVI, iv (1954), 554-564 and XVII, iii (1955), 383-407.

——, *The New Criticism* (Norfolk, Connecticut, 1941).

——, *The World's Body* (New York, 1938).

Richards, I. A., *Coleridge on Imagination* (New York, 1934).

——, *The Philosophy of Rhetoric* (Oxford, 1936).

——, *Practical Criticism: A Study of Literary Judgment* (London, 1929).

——, *Principles of Literary Criticism* (New York, 1925).

——, *Science and Poetry* (New York, 1926).

——, and C. K. Ogden, *The Meaning of Meaning* (London, 1923).

—— with C. K. Ogden and James Wood, *The Foundations of Aesthetics* (New York, 1925).

Stanford, W. B., *Greek Metaphor: Studies in Theory and Practice* (Oxford, 1936).

Stevens, Wallace, *Poems by Wallace Stevens* (New York, 1957).

Tate, Allen, ed., *The Language of Poetry* (Princeton, 1942).

——, *The Man of Letters in the Modern World* (New York, 1955).

Wellek, René, and Austin Warren, *Theory of Literature* (New York, 1942, revised 1955).

Wells, Henry W., *Poetic Imagery: Illustrated from Eliabethan Literature* (New York, 1961).

Whalley, George, *Poetic Process* (London, 1953).

Wheelwright, Philip, *Metaphor and Reality* (Bloomington, 1962).

Wimsatt, W. K., Jr., and Monroe C. Beardsley, *The Verbal Icon: Studies in the Meaning of Poetry* (Lexington, Kentucky, 1954).

——, and Cleanth Brooks, *Literary Criticism: A Short History* (New York, 1964).

INDEX

DE PROPRIETATIBUS LITTERARUM

edited by
C. H. VAN SCHOONEVELD

Series Maior

1. Marcus B. Hester, *The Meaning of Poetic Metaphor: An Analysis in the Light of Wittgenstein's Claim that Meaning is Use.* 1967. 229 pp.
ƒ 36.— / $ 10.00

2. Rodney Delasanta, *The Epic Voice.* 1967. 140 pp.   ƒ 22.— / $ 5.75

3. Bennison Gray, *Style: The Problem and its Solution.* 1969. 117 pp.
ƒ 23.— / $ 6.50

5. Raimund Belgardt, *Romantische Poesie: Begriff und Bedeutung bei Friedrich Schlegel.* 1970. 257 pp.   ƒ 45.— / $ 12.50

Series Minor

1. Trevor Eaton, *The Semantics of Literature.* 1966. 72 pp.
ƒ 10.— / $ 2.80

2. Walter A. Koch, *Recurrence and a Three-Modal Approach to Poetry.* 1966. 57 pp.   ƒ 10.— / $ 2.80

3. Nancy Sullivan, *Perspective and the Poetic Process.* 1968. 56 pp.
ƒ 10.— / $ 2.80

4. Donald LoCicero, *Novellentheorie: The Practicality of the Theoretical.* 1970. 120 pp.   ƒ 16.— / $ 4.50

Series Practica

1. Robert G. Cohn, *Mallarmé's Masterpiece: New Findings.* 1966. 114 pp.
ƒ 22.— / $ 5.75

2. Constance B. Hieatt, *The Realism of Dream Vision: The Poetic Exploitation of the Dream-Experience in Chaucer and His Contemporaries.* 1967. 112 pp.   ƒ 16.—

3. Joseph J. Mogan Jr., *Chaucer and the Theme of Mutability.* 1969. 190 pp.   ƒ 26.— / $ 7.45

4. Peter Nusser, *Musils Romantheorie.* 1967. 114 pp.   ƒ 18.— / $ 5.00

5. Marjorie Perloff, *Rhyme and Meaning in the Poetry of Yeats.* 1970. 249 pp.   ƒ 48.— / $ 13.75

6. Marian H. Cusac, *Narrative Structure in the Novels of Sir Walter Scott.* 1969. 128 pp.   ƒ 20.— / $ 5.75

7. Victor Wortley, *Tallement des Réaux: The Man through his Style*. 1969. 99 pp.   *f* 22.— / $ 6.30

9. Donald R. Swanson, *Three Conquerors: Character and Method in the Mature Works of George Meredith*. 1969. 148 pp.   *f* 22.— / $ 6.30

10. Irwin Gopnik, *A Theory of Style and Richardson's Clarissa*. 1970. 140 pp.   *f* 22.—

12. Sylvia D. Feldman, *The Morality-Patterned Comedy of the Renaissance*. 1971. 165 pp.   *f* 18.— / $ 5.00

13. Giles Mitchell, *The Art Theme in Joyce Cary's First Trilogy*. 1971. 136 pp.   *f* 18.— / $ 5.00

17. Meredith B. Raymond, *Swinburne's Poetics: Theory and Practice*. 1971. 202 pp.   *f* 36.—

20. Edgar B. Schick, *Metaphorical Organicism in Herder's Early Works: A Study of the Relation of Herder's Literary Idiom to His World-view*. 1971. 135 pp.   *f* 25.— / $ 6.95

22. James E. Magner Jr., *John Crowe Ransom: Critical Principles and Pre-occupations*. 1971. 134 pp.   *f* 18.— / $ 5.00

23. Elisabeth Th. M. van de Laar, *The Inner Structure of Wuthering Heights: A Study of an Imaginative Field*. 1969. 262 pp.
                                                                       f 36.— / $ 10.00

24. Bernard L. Einbond, *Samuel Johnson's Allegory*. 1971. 104 pp.
                                                                       f 18.— / $ 5.00

27. Richard Vernier, *'Poésie ininterrompue' et la poétique de Paul Eluard*. 1971. 180 pp.   *f* 25.— / $ 6.95
28. Hugh L. Hennedy, *Unity in Barsetshire*. 1971. 144 pp. *f* 28.—

35. Roman Jakobson and Lawrence G. Jones, *Shakespeare's Verbal Art in Th'Expence of Spirit*. 1970. 32 pp.   *f* 10.— / $ 2.90

MOUTON · PUBLISHERS · THE HAGUE